Science

for All

2nd Edition
Revised by
Les Jones
and Sue Skelton

**MEC TEACHER
FELLOWS**

Sue Fagg and
Sue Skelton
in association with
**Pam Aherne and
Ann Thornber**

1993

David Fulton Publishers Ltd
2 Barbon Close, London WC1N 3JX

First published in Great Britain by
David Fulton Publishers, 1990
Second Edition 1993

British LIbrary of Cataloguing in Publication Data
Skelton, Sue
  1.Science for all
  1.Science
  I.Title   II.Fagg, Sue
  500

  ISBN 1-85346-256-X

Printed in Great Britain by Bell and Bain Ltd., Glasgow

Contents

> **NB**   AT 3 strand (ii) is not represented at key stage 1 and 2
> AT 3 strand (iv) is not represented at levels 1 and 2

List of Figures

Acknowledgements

Our thanks go to the many colleagues in working groups across the country too numerous to mention, who have given up their time to read our work and offer their advice and expertise. In particular we thank Peter Mittler, the staff of the six Manchester schools for pupils with severe and complex learning difficulties and the Manchester Science Team who have responded on a regular basis to the development of this work.

Our warmest thanks go to the pupils we teach with whom we enjoy science as an integral part of every day's learning.

We acknowledge Vic Johnson whose skill, dedication and patience in computer technology has made the first edition of this document so effective as an educational resources.

Finally we wish to thank Linda Bardsley, St James' Primary School, Pat Derbyshire, Crosby Meadow School, Barbara Devlin, Gorton Brook First School, Sue Fagg, Lancashire County Council Advisory Service, Irene Heggarty, Manchester City Council Inspection and Advisory Service, Sarah Kameena, Judith Sebba, Cambridge Institute of Education, Rodney House School, Mary Whalley, Piper Hill School for advice and support during the redrafting and updating of this edition.

Introduction

This document analyses Science in the National Curriculum and has been updated in line with the revised Science National Curriculum format (1991). It follows on from the work which was developed by MEC Teacher Fellows in 1990, illustrating that the education offered to ALL pupils irrespective of need, can and indeed should include the National Curriculum. Every pupil therefore is seen to be working within level 1 or above. (See Entitlement for All in practice (1990) Fagg, Aherne, Skelton and Thornber; Communication for All and Mathematics for All, Aherne, Thornber, Fagg and Skelton (1990a and b).

The following quote taken from NCC Curriculum Guidance 9 (1992), postively demonstrates that the term 'A Curriculum for All' is sytematically taking shape in other relevant and nationally produced publications.

> *'Use of the term "within level 1"*
>
> *Pupils should be described as working within PoS relating to level*
>
> *1 until they have achieved the SoA at this level. They then move*
>
> *on to working within the PoS relating to level 2. Planning and*
>
> *implementation of daily activities should refer to pupils as work-*
>
> *ing within the key stage PoS relevant to their needs.'*
>
> **NCC Curriculum Guidance 9.**

The document will help all those concerned with the education of pupils with severe and complex learning difficulties gain insight into the vital importance of Science as a core curricular area. The content will specifically assist the classroom teacher to give all pupils access to a broad science curriculum.

It is the clear intention of this document to describe progression through level 1 and level 2. The programme of study has been expanded and the milestones identified within levels of the Statements of Attainment.

Attainment Target 1, Scientific investigation, is addressed in detail. This attainment target is the most important procedure through which pupils explore science.

The work incorporates some ideas for record keeping and assessment. The style of record keeping a school uses for science is a decision for each school and is likely to reflect their schemes of work and be in line with record keeping in other subjects.

The content of the document is based as far as possible on existing good practice in special and mainstream schools where a broad, balanced, relevant and differentiated curriculum is offered.

A framework has been provided, within which pupils with special educational needs can continue to make genuine progress through the National Curriculum, Science.

Science for Pupils with Special Educational Needs

Since the introduction of the National Curriculum, Science, and publication of the first edition of 'Science for All' much progress has been made in the area of science for pupils with special educational needs. Whilst complacency would be at least unwise, experience has been gained by teachers in this field. The bibliography to this document lists some recent documents, amongst which NCC Curriculum Guidance 9 and 10 are particularly valuable.

The National Primary Survey (NPS) in 1978 found that one of the greatest obstacles to the teaching of science was the lack of science knowledge on the part of primary teachers. Her Majesty's Inspectorate reported in The Teaching and Learning of Science (1989) an increase in the amount of science taught ten years later. This improvement was believed in part to be due to Education Support Grants being used to provide inservice training. Some local education authorities included special schools in this type of inservice whilst others did not. Consequently many teachers in special schools may still lack confidence about their scientific knowledge.

Many institutes of higher education offer a 20 day science course for science coordinators – primary schools. These courses are designed to explore the knowledge and understanding described in AT 2, 3 and 4 that many teachers from primary and special backgrounds find challenging within the framework of overall demands regarding curriculum. These courses are administered by Local Education Authorities and are open to teachers from special schools.

The Importance of Planning

Teachers planning scientific work for pupils with severe and complex learning difficulties should have a clear grasp of the scientific knowledge they wish a pupil or group of pupils to grasp. The following work gives information that can act as a guide to teachers when planning science for pupils whose progress within the attainment targets may be centred around level 1 or 2. The programmes of study and milestones associated with each attainment target should not be seen in isolation but provide support for the individual pupil and their teacher within the school's scheme of work.

'A scheme of work is a written statement which describes the work

planned for pupils within a class or group over a specific period...

Each scheme of work is part of the 5–16 continuum and, taken with

preceding and subsequent schemes, will describe the detailed

curriculum structure for science for pupils across all key stages.'

NCC (1989c) Science NonStatutory Guidance.

The scheme of work may include fixed or open topics or themes, depending on whether or not staff have a choice regarding the work carried out as in 'open' or no choice 'fixed'. Senior pupils may have their scientific learning experiences planned through modules, or projects. TVEI (Technical and Vocational Educational Initiative) has been used by some special schools to facilitate a rapid move to delivering the curriculum through a modular approach. Whatever the approach the scheme of work should ensure pupils participate in a varied scientific curriculum. The use of a spiral curriculum model (Figure 1) helps the consolidation of learning without excessive repetition.

NCC Curriculum Guidance, document 10, emphasises the importance of planning the teaching and learning of science at three levels:

• whole school policy;

• class schemes of work;

• groups and individual activity plans.

It then goes on to describe, in some detail, how specific parts of programmes of study relating to AT2, 3 or 4 might be accessed through AT1. It also describes how some activities were modified for individual children with special educational needs.

Although it only draws upon a small part of the programme of study examples are given for each key stage. A planning check list is included.

The issue of planning science lessons is also explored, in some detail and very effectively, in Curriculum Guidance 9 (The National Curriculum and Pupils with Severe Learning Difficulties). A useful strategy for planning at the level of whole key stages is described in 'First Steps to Curriculum Organisation – key stage 1 and 2' available from Manchester City Council Education Department.

Science must be seen as an integral part of the whole curriculum and planning through a topic that encompasses all curricular areas allows this. Entitlement for All in Practice (Fagg, Agherne, Skelton and Thornber 1990) illustrates this integrated cohesive approach to learning. English, Mathematics and Technology are frequently incorporated into a science based activity. The National Curriculum: Making it Work in the Primary School (Association for Science Education 1989) illustrates well the interrelated aspects of the National Curriculum documents which must not be seen as isolated areas of learning.

'Science is in a unique position as compared with Mathematics

and English in that it can be approached in a motivating, exciting

manner making total use of a scientific investigation. This can

often be free of any restraints of reading, writing, calculating or

reporting. If the activity is carefully chosen, the pupils might well want to "communicate" with each other about it, by talking, arguing etc. They can make a model, a diagram or picture of their findings which is a non threatening way of doing Mathematics and English.'

A. Jones (1990)

If progression is to be ensured pupils need to build steadily on their achievements. This progression should be carefully monitored especially within the scientific investigations. In attainment targets involving scientific knowledge, some of which may not be experienced regularly, achievements a pupil makes in one term may not be retained until the next. While this lack of learning retention is true of many pupils, it is far more significant among the group of pupils to whom this document is addressed. The spiral curriculum as illustrated in Figure 1, where pupils regularly revisit areas of learning, helps to overcome this difficulty, pupils regaining and retaining knowledge when it is presented through a variety of topics and contexts incorporated in the schemes of work.

The organisation and management of differentiated teaching, learning and assessment strategies, for specific pupils, is the essential process in making progress a reality.

'Differentiation is the process by which curriculum objectives, teaching methods, assessment methods, resources and learning activities are planned to cater for the needs of individual pupils.'

(Science and Pupils with Special Educational Needs – a workshop pack for key stages 1 and 2, NCC).

This document describes differentiation by task and by outcome. Three INSET activities are described which all teachers would find invaluable.

'As humans we are curious about the environment we live in.'

NCC (1989c) Science NonStatutory Guidance.

Education can foster, stimulate and develop this curiosity through science.

Figure 1   A Spiral Curriculum Model

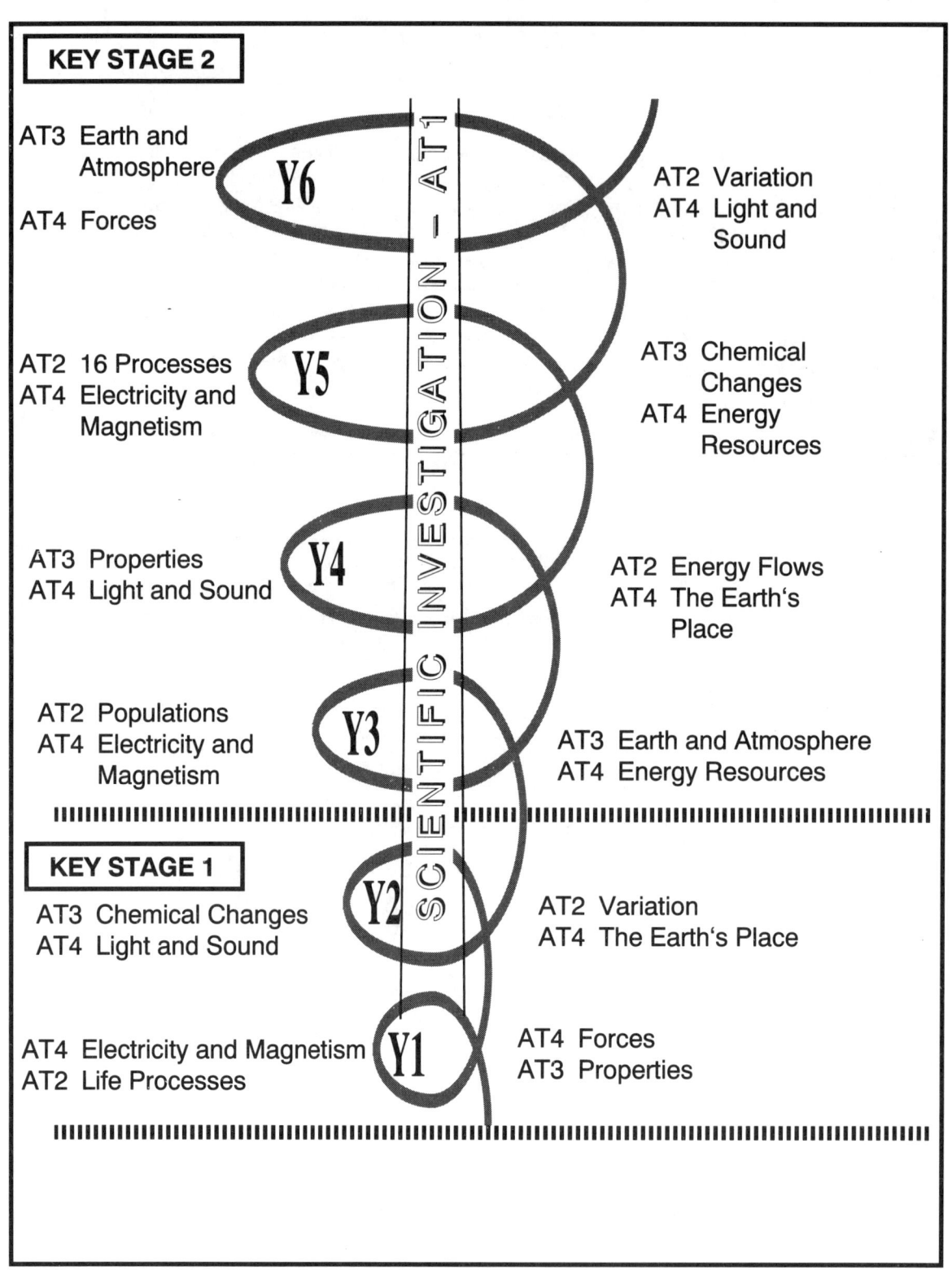

This diagram represents the model of the Spiral Curriculum. However, it should not be seen as an accurate example. Most strands of the attainment targets will be visited and re-visited much more often than they appear to be in this diagram.

The Organisation of the National Curriculum 1991

The main revision of the National Curriculum Science (1989) was to reduce the statements of attainment from 407 to 176. The number of attainment targets was also reduced from 17 to 4. However, the content remains largely unchanged. Old attainment targets reappear as strands of new attainment targets. This chart illustrates the relationship between the two:

1989 Attainment targets	1991 Attainment targets and strands	Comments
1	1 i, ii, iii	Scientific investigation
2	2 ii	Inheritance and evolution – variation and classification have been combined with old AT4 into this single strand
	2 iii	Populations – factors affecting population size have been combined with old AT5 into this single strand.
	2 iv	Cycles of matter and energy
3	2 i	Life processes – health education references are in PoS only
4	2 ii	Combined with part of old AT2 into this single strand
5	2 iii	Combined with part of old AT2 into this single strand
6	3 i	Properties, classification and structure of materials
7	3 iii	Chemical changes
8	3 ii	Explanations of the properties of materials
9	3 iv	Earth and atmosphere – some overlap with National Curriculum geography removed

10	4 iii	Forces and their effects
11	4 i	Electricity and magnetism
12	4 i	This strand includes knowledge and applications of microelectronic components and systems; use of IT devices in investigations is now in PoS for AT1
13	4 ii	Energy resources and energy transfer
14	4 iv	Combined with old AT15 into this single strand called light and sound
15	4 iv	Combined with old AT14 into this single strand called light and sound
16	4 v	Earth's place in the Universe
17	1 iii	This strand includes interpreting results and evaluation of scientific evidence the history of scientific ideas is included in the PoS for ATs 2–4

Further clarification can be gained by reference to Science, Nonstatutory Guidance 1991.

How the Programmes of Study and Associated Attainment Targets have been expanded incorporating Notes of Guidance on the Milestone Steps

It is perhaps obvious, but still essential to restate that it is to the programmes of study to which teachers should turn when they plan the education of the pupils in their schools.

The programme of study for each key stage have been considered and their content expanded, in light of recent developments in the field of science education and the curiculum traditionally offered in schools for pupils with severe and complex learning difficulties.

Each attainment target has been studied and milestone steps, illustrated wtih examples, suggested for each statement of attainment whilst the milestones may present as a developmental checklist, they should rather be treated as a guide or framework that acknowledges developmental stages of learning. It is not an intention that each step be learned before moving on to the next. **The aim in numbering the milestones has been to provide a consistent measure for all steps, eg the milestones numbered 3 in attainment target 1 level 1 are roughly equivalent to other level 1 milestone 3 steps in other attainment targets.** The variation in the context of some of the statements of attainment has made this consistency within the levels difficult to achieve. With this in mind, the breakdown of the statements of attainment for level 1 do not always start at step 1 as it was felt in some instances they could not be broken down to a sufficiently early developmental level. **Some statements of attainment, where the content is less extensive than that included in others, have fewer milestones but the ones suggested are numbered according to their difficulty eg a statement of attainment may have only 3 milestone steps 1 a 1, 1 a 3, 1 a 5.**

The pages have been arranged in a similar style to the National Curriculum, Science, 1991. The statements of attainment and examples generally face the programme of study at the same level. It is hoped that this format makes the document easier to use in planning classroom activities. However, since the programmes of study are more general and wide ranging, the levels indicated are only a guide. A review of the programmes of study across levels 1 and 2 will generally be more informative than simply to cross check from milestones to programmes of study.

Suggested Programmes of Study & Milestones relating to all the Attainment Targets

The programmes of study in the National Curriculum, Science, 1991, begin with a general introduction which explores communication and science in everyday life.

Communication

Communication in science requires pupils to develop reporting, questioning and interactive skills. The development of communication for pupils with severe and complex learning difficulties is associated with all areas of learning. A more detailed account of this work as it relates to National Curriculum can be read in 'Communication for All' (Aherne, Thornber, Fagg and Skelton 1990a). Within this document it is appropriate to highlight those areas most readily developed within the field of science.

Activities should include opportunities to:

• work in pairs or small groups which encourage the development of communication skills eg one pupil has to instruct the other how to carry out an activity, one pupil has to describe the contents of a feely bag to the other, a group have to decide what criteria to use for sorting materials.

• follow instructions as an individual.

• play guessing games eg what is in my hand that is cold and drips – ice. (These activities help to foster the ability to hypothesise and predict.)

• contribute in discussions, listening as well as communicating ideas.

• report back as an individual or with others to an adult and/or other pupils about an investigation. (Initially such reporting will take place while the activity is still taking place, but as skills develop reporting after the activity may be possible.)

When participating in scientific activities all forms of communication (total communication) should be accepted and encouraged as this is likely to lead to the greatest achievements. More detailed reporting can be given by utilising gestures, facial expression, postures, drawings, computer printouts as well as vocalisation and speech. Pupils should be encouraged to develop their own communication skills but they should also be encouraged to utilise each others skills, gaining greater skill and confidence from a group approach.

This area is explored in detail in NCC Curriculum Guidance 9.

Throughout all activities communication should be fostered. However, for those pupils whose progress in this area is severely impeded this should not prevent in any way their access to a broad scientific experience and curriculum. Perhaps it is this group of pupils, for example those who have complex learning difficulties and severe problems of social adjustment and thus may find little apparent reward in communicating with adults or pupils, who present the greatest challenge.

Science in everyday life

'As pupils begin to mature and gain increasing knowledge and

understanding they should be given the opportunity to develop an awareness of the importance of science in everyday life including its relevance to personal health and safety. This awareness should be encouraged through visits. Pupils should use a variety of domestic and environmental contexts as starting points for learning science.'

National Curriculum, 1991.

There is a great progression through attainment target levels which aims to take pupils from the familiar and the everyday to the abstract and the scientific. Since the majority of pupils with severe and complex learning difficulties will be working within levels 1 and 2 they are unlikely to make significant progress towards the abstract and the scientific. The importance of science in everyday life is then much more important to the pupils in question.

In addition, respect for each individual's actual age irrespective of their level of study and degree of maturity must be acknowledged through the use of age appropriate materials in age appropriate settings.

The emphasis on personal and social development already established in the curriculum in the areas of personal independence and independence in the community, will complement the areas of access to science in everyday life.

Procedure and content, AT 1 and its relationship to ATs 2, 3 and 4

The National Curriculum, science, at Key stage 1 and 2 is described in official documentation as 50% AT 1 and 50% ATs 2, 3 and 4. This is reflected in aggregation guidance for end of key stage assessment procedures. These attainment targets are interelated. AT 1 provides a procedure through which to explore ATs 2, 3 and 4, which in turn provides a context in which to develop AT 1. However, AT 1 is complex and demanding, even at levels 1 and 2. Learning needs to be organised so that pupils have opportunities to develop procedure skills *in their own right*.

Since, perhaps by definition, Teachers of children with learning difficulties, are particularly concerned with learning procedure rather than simply content, AT 1 provides the fundamental starting point for planning teaching and learning activities.

Attainment Target 1:
Scientific investigation

Pupils should develop the intellectual and practical skills which will allow them to explore and investigate the world of science and develop a fuller understanding of scientific phenomena, the nature of the theories explaining these, and the procedures of scientific investigation. This should take place through activities that require a progessively more systematic and quantified approach which develops and draws upon an increasing knowledge and understanding of science. The activities should encourage the ability to plan and carry out investigations in which pupils:

i)   ask questions, predict and hypothesise;

ii)   observe, measure and manipulate variables;

iii)   interpret their results and evaluate scientific evidence.

Suggested programme of study leading to the achievement of AT 1

Level 1

*   Learning experiences to assist the development of all the senses.

Some pupils have sensory impairments. Some pupils have a physical disability which inhibits free exploration or may reduce the tactile awareness of parts of the body. Pupils with profound and multiple learning difficulties frequently have sensory impairments that limit their all round development. Work in this attainment target will be based on the development of the senses in the early stages. For pupils with impairments it is vital to carefully structure this area of learning where differentiation and experience both play a valuable role.

To enable intervention programmes to be planned more easily the areas of sensory development to be considered – auditory, visual, kinaesthetic and olfactory awareness – are outlined in separate areas as this will enable planning to meet the needs of pupils with impairments. The development of the senses should not be seen in isolation as together they help the individual make sense of their world. Programmes for the development of the senses where there is an impairment should be developed in conjunction with other specialists in the area eg teacher of the visually impaired, teacher of the hearing impaired, physiotherapist and speech therapist. Biograms may be utilised to record the response of some pupils with profound and multiple handicaps to different stimuli. Pupils need to experience learning in a reactive environment where their actions are likely to cause changes around them.

Hearing, sound and auditory discrimination

Activities should include opportunities to:

*   have passive experiences of gentle simple sounds eg during close communication, involving speech and song (the adult ensuring time and space is left for the individual's response), clear sound, music, toys and musical instruments which offer a variation in pitch.

- experience of own noises both vocal and those caused through movement, to which built in feedback is ensured eg movement of body part in contact with a silver foil survival bag (normally used on outdoor pursuit expeditions).

- feel the vibratory sources of sound eg voice box, mouth, body.

- experience with a reassuring adult and respond to, a variety of sounding toys and objects, musical experiences including live music, tapes, situations involving variation in sound levels assisting the individual to tolerate new sounds eg assembly, hydrotherapy pool, main dining area. These experiences should be alternated with periods of silence.

- make sounds eg use of simple switch to activate a tape, bells attached to body parts, sounding toy or instrument placed so pupil can initiate a sound.

- locate source of sound by head/eye turn, touch, (Note this process is progresive from midline, to above, to below, to behind the ears.)

- experience vocalisations, own and others, encouraging intentional sound interaction and imitation.

- experience sounds produced through play and body movement (intentional and nonintentional noises), built in feedback to movement eg pupil is placed on a mat, plain or pictorial that is sensitive to movement throughout or in parts.

- experience sounds made within the school, local community and in a variety of settings eg countryside, concert hall. Encourage a reaction to these sounds and communicate about them.

- listen to sound in context and communicate a reaction in an interactive exchange.

- make sounds using a diverse range of equipment eg spoon on a table, in a pan, beans in a tin etc.

- experience listening to or making sounds for a partner, sound games that encourage interaction (Manchester Education Committee 1989b – Me and Others.)

Some pupils have hearing impairments and the specialist teacher of the hearing impaired should always be consulted closely to advise and assist when developing education programmes and activities for these pupils. Their knowledge will frequently benefit other pupils particularly when developing this area of the curriculum. The pupil with hearing impairment must always be given appropriate support if using hearing aids and consideration must be given within the educational environment to ensure sound distractions are erased by the use of carpets etc.

Further ideas

- experience of environments where sound varies distinctively, eg hall, outdoor area – paved and grass, kitchen, office, hydrotherapy/swimming pool, roadside are all useful resources and immediately available.

- sound should not be provided out of context in early developmental stages but used to assist a pupil to associate a familiar noise with a familiar event. In early stages of development this noise may be emphasised or contrived to help learning, eg music always being played for ten minutes after morning drinks when a rest period is given.

- as pupils develop their ability to listen, opportunities to share communication verbally, by gesture or body movement needs to be provided. Does silence exist? What sounds do trees make? What sounds do we make?

Sight, visual acuity

Activities should include opportunities to:

- be positioned to gain eye contact with others and to look at objects. (The pupil should be positioned at different angles, in dark and light using natural and artificial light.)

- experience visually stimulating objects – close to and distant from, to assist the development of fixation and horizontal and vertical tracking (Manchester Education Committee undated – The Programme Planner for Blind and Partially Sighted Children of Lower Ability).

- experience looking at others near by to see facial expression and thus enhance communication skills by shared mutual interest and rejection (purposeful change in gaze).

- learn visually directed reaching and the manipulation of a variety of objects/ toys that incorporate variation in shape, size, colour and reflective properties (this enhances hand eye co-ordination).

- choose objects/toys to use/play with based on visual cue. Experience of interacting with other pupils and adults through facial expression and body position encouraging mutual regard and interaction through visual response, self directed physical contact and verbalisation.

- use vision to observe an activity, object, scene and to communicate details regarding what has been seen as well as a response to what has been seen.

- observe their local environment being encouraged to take a visual interest in all that is going on round about them (MEC 1989d – Me and My Surroundings).

Pupils who are still in the early stages of developing their observation skills should be positioned or encouraged to move to different parts of the room where a variety of different light situations or visually stimulating materials area available. Care must be taken not to provide an environment that is confusing to a child, confusion may be caused by an excess of mobiles, or if the child is given too many objects and toys to play with.

Activities involving direct development of vision are useful for pupils with visual impairment and for those working within an early developmental level. Visual tracking may need to be developed and can be assisted by following a structured programme devised in consultation with a teacher of the visually impaired. A specific environment may be used for this work eg a light booth. Other pupils can use this type of resource for experimental work involving light. (See Betts F. 1992, Chapman E. and Stone J. 1988)

Toys and displays should be chosen to enhance visual interest.

Staff working with pupils should position themselves to ensure good eye contact is possible. **This is vital** for pupils with profound and multiple learning difficulties and for those who have difficulty relating to others. Later development is assisted by staff ensuring the pupil can easily move their visual awareness from one area of observation to the person they are communicating with. Mobile pupils can often find diversity of visual experience during general exploration.

Planning the classroom should incorporate the opportunity to enhance visual interest and thus encourage observation and communication. Areas of learning should be set up to avoid distractions from other sections of the room, if areas are visually attractive a pupil is likely to explore the activities available within that area.

The common practice of painting on classroom windows discourages pupils from looking outside and observing the daily changes in the local environment. The view from a window in the rural and urban environment offers a never ending opportunity to observe changes in the weather, the effect of light on the buildings or fields, who or what can be seen, the opportunity to hypothesise about what might be seen.

Such observations also have the benefit of having no resource implications.

Kinaesthetic awareness

Activities should include the opportunities to:

- experience different physical positions eg flat and sloping surfaces, still and vibrating surfaces.

- experience being placed on different tactile surfaces eg smooth or rough surface, cool like plastic, warm like sheepskin. (The activity needs to be paced to allow each pupil time to react and communicate their reaction to the sensations.)

- experience coactive movement, ie a pupil enjoying moving with help from a familiar adult through massage, vibration, movement sessions, use of a ball pool and movement in warm water. (See also programmes of study leading to the achievement of level 1 Mathematics for All Aherne, Thornber, Fagg, Skelton 1990b.)

- feel a variety of materials – liquid and solid to enhance tactile awareness and whole body movement. Experience of food of different textures and consistencies.

- participate in active movement involving the whole body. Such movement can be assisted for pupils with physical disabilities by the use of blankets to swing pupils in, by staff moving with a pupil in water and on apparatus eg a wide slide.

- work with a variety of tactile materials to develop touch eg when involved in creative activities, exploration in sand, stones, shells, when using play/leisure equipment etc.

- move within the school environment and the local community including the use of park play equipment, escalators, lifts, buses, trains, boats, trampolines, pushing equipment eg buggies.

- explore a variety of materials freely available within the classroom environment eg science table containing materials that feel rough and smooth, a home corner that includes plasticine, play doh, pasta, beans, dressing up clothes from different cultural backgrounds, variety of bedding materials for a dolls cot, classroom shop. (In some cases access to some materials may only be able to be provided when an adult is available to supervise thus ensuring unsuitable materials are not eaten.)

- develop movement: in water, on a variety of terrains, on PE apparatus, to music, on bikes etc.

- sort objects by touch, feeling using different parts of the body, feeling bag activities (MEC 1989 b – Me and Others).

When developing this area of work, consideration needs to be given to a pupil's physical ability, any physical impairment being taken into consideration. A physical impairment can lead to lack of mobility, lack of feeling in limbs or areas of the body. Those with physical limitation must be assisted in their exploration. Programmes of work should be developed in consultation with the professionals supporting the pupil eg physiotherapist, occupational therapist, school nurse. Such consultation will ensure the pupil is receiving education in a holistic manner all working towards the same physical goals.

Although movement and the development of touch through tactile experiences are considered separately, within the teaching situation these will often be intertwined and inseparable. For example, when doing massage, the body is stimulated through the touch of the masseur and the oil they are using as well as developing the mobility of a part of the body.

This work is vital to assist a pupil to develop an awareness of all their body parts. The pupil who has no apparent physical disability may suffer from poor coordination resulting in clumsy movement. A programme based on the above can therefore assist in the development of body awareness.

Smell and taste – olfactory awareness

Activities should include opportunities to:

- experience and react to a variety of smells occurring in the immediate vicinity eg cooking, bathing.

- experience and react to a variety of mild flavours in food.

- experience a variety of smells introduced in context, near the nasal passages and in the immediate vicinity. Time should be given to show a positive response which can then be acted upon as a potentially communicative behaviour.

- taste a variety of distinct flavours in food and drink at appropriate times during the day eg snack time, lunch time.

- interact with objects that have a variety of smells.

- respond differentially to alternative drinks or foods with distinctive tastes and through this activity learn early from choice making skills.

- participate in experiences that involve a variety of smells and tastes eg celebrations – Divali, Chinese New Year, Christmas (me and Others MEC 1989b).

- experiment with the production of tastes and smells through cookery, creative work using herbs and flavourings.

The classroom can offer the opportunity for individual investigation into taste and smell by an area being devoted to this, pupils being encouraged to bring in examples from home, sorting into pleasant and unpleasant smells and tastes based on individual preference. The home corner can also be used to offer a variety of smells. Bathing, changing and areas used for personal grooming should incorporate a variety of the smells experienced and promote personal choice in this area (Longhorn 1988).

Consultation with parents in this area of development is essential if a true picture of a pupil's experience or sensitivity to smell and taste is to be appreciated. Some pupils will require an intense experience or sensation to gain from this area of work due to impairment in areas of the nervous system, others may be very sensitive and if care is not taken progress will not be made. At all times a pupil's response must be noted and the activity stopped if discomfort is shown.

When developing a pupil's interest in taste great care must be taken to avoid sweet drinks and food that could encourage the development of a sweet tooth and subsequent tooth decay (the school dentist and dental nurse can give advice in this area).

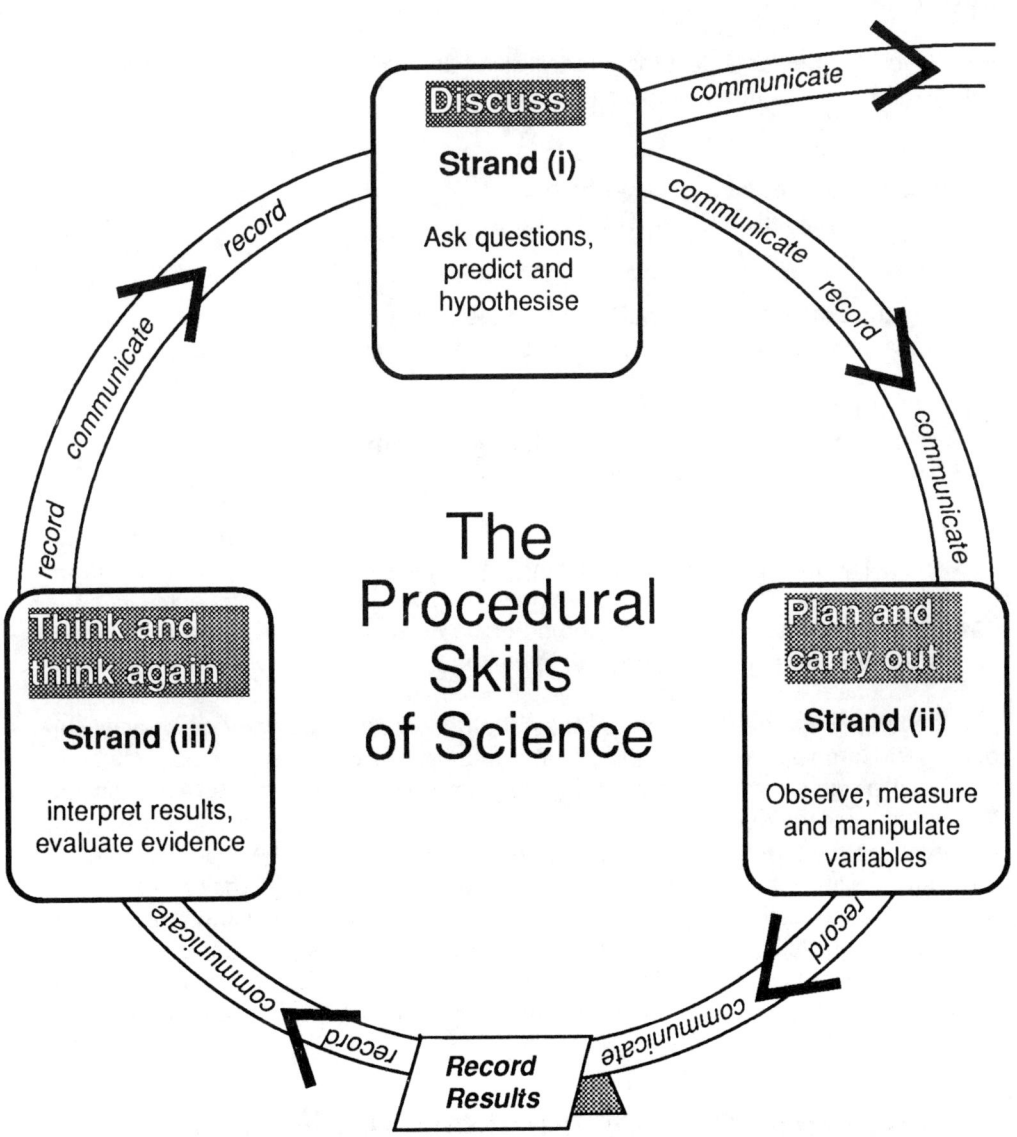

Attainment Target 1: Scientific investigation

Suggested programme of study leading to the achievement of AT 1

Level 2

At level 2 of Sc 1 pupils' ability to think and plan scientifically is beginning to be developed. Although progress for pupils with severe and complex learning difficulties will be very gradual, **it is vital** this area of learning is planned carefully to ensure progression. Successful learning within all other attainment targets is linked with achievements in this area.

Sc 1 covers the fundamental procedural skills of Science. Its statements of attainment can be grouped into three interrelated strands:

Strand (i)
ask questions, predict and hypothesise
which has been labelled DISCUSS

Strand (ii)
observe, measure and manipulate variables
which has been labelled PLAN AND CARRY OUT

Strand (iii)
interpret their results and evaluate scientific evidence
which has been labelled THINK AND THINK AGAIN

The three strands refer to the statements of attainment against which children will be assessed. The HDERIC model described in previous Manchester publications and based on the 1989 National Curriculum document is completely compatible with the 1991 attainment targets and programmes of study. However, the current document orders group statements of attainment in a different way.

This document has been written to reflect the new statements and how they will be assessed. Complete investigations are often inappropriate at levels 1 and 2. However, the loop of procedural skills can form a strategy for planning and learning experiences. Within this strategy questions are raised, experiences are planned and carried out, observations made and interpreted. Figure 2 shows the cyclical way in which these three strands link into each other. The interpretations and evaluations of one investigation can suggest ideas and hypotheses for another. This is why the thread leads away to the right. Although the recording of results and the communicating of ideas are not part of the statements of attainment, they appear in the programme of study, they are clearly aspects of procedural skills and as such they appear in our diagram.

Strand (i) Discuss – ask questions, predict and hypothesise

Activities should include opportunities to:

•   questions adults and each other about why or how things happen, eg why was swimming cancelled? Why did the custard taste burnt?

- play/experiment with equipment which fosters the desire to ask why and how things happen, eg hang items on springs, mix water with quantities of sand, salt, flour, plaster of Paris.

- participate in activities that require a pupil to hypothesise and predict in conjunction with staff. Outdoor pursuits offer the opportunity to predict whether surfaces will be slippery or not due to the weather conditions, wet rock is not safe for climbing, walking on wet stones requires more care than dry.

- hypothesise, make predictions about a situation/event/activity before it takes place (encouragement being given to any comments, gesture that indicates possible outcomes).

- seek solutions to their own questions and those posed by others.

- answer their own questions when asking questions of 'what will happen if'. Pupils should be encouraged to follow this style of questioning through.

- **encourage pupils to use and develop their scientific knowledge and understanding.**

- **involve pupils and their teachers in promoting ideas and seeking solutions.**

The school has to be organised to ensure all staff appreciate the need to give pupils the time to question. Questioning for pupils who have difficulty relating to others, delayed language development or articulation difficulties is not as natural an occurrence as it is for many young children and needs careful fostering. Pupils who feel they are in an unsympathetic environment are unlikely to persevere with the development of questioning skills they find very difficult. Without such questioning many opportunities for learning will be lost.

Pupils should be encouraged to take responsibility for their own activities enabling them to predict more readily what can happen if certain criteria are not fulfilled. Everyday school routines should be used eg collection of drink, returning dirty items to appropriate area at lunchtime, personal responsibility for remembering swimming costume and towel. If pupils are encouraged to really follow through these responsibilities the consequences of actions will be more readily understood, eg dirty cups left on a table that is needed for other work is difficult, no towel after swimming is very uncomfortable – alternative item for drying has to be found.

Activities that have startling results help pupils to question through gesture, vocalisation or speech. Science can easily be presented in a stimulating and exciting form that assists in fostering this vital area of development in communication. Throughout activities there is the possibility of developing the forum for questioning, hypothesising and predicting. For pupils with very limited communication staff working in close liaison with them during an activity can foster this, initially introducing the idea themselves of making hypotheses and predictions.

This area of development is closely linked with communication.

Strand (ii) Plan and carry out – observe, measure and manipulate variables

(a) Planning and designing investigations

Activities should include opportunities to:

- experiment/play freely with equipment altering the way it is set out, adding to the equipment and taking items away eg in the class shop – utilising a variety of methods for weighing items, scales with weights, stones, basic balance.

- plan their own equipment for activities throughout the school day, encouraging them to take responsibility for items required to complete an activity eg choice of suitable bag for carrying heavy load of shopping, has the strength been checked?

- plan trying activities in different situations eg bouncing balls on hard and soft surfaces, on surfaces at different angles, making FAIR TESTS of balls or surfaces.

- try to solve a set problem by planning and designing an investigation alone or in conjunction with others, eg which car can travel the longest distance on the hall floor, how long does it take to boil a soft centred egg.

- **encourage an appreciation of the need for safe and careful action.**

Whenever possible pupils should be given access to equipment individually or in very small groups. Practical personal experience is needed to help pupils with severe and complex learning difficulties plan and design. Frequently real situations occurring throughout the day may be used to help the development of this concept, planning how to pour drinks out so all have a drink, planning how to decide when biscuits are cooked and finding out what they are like after shorter and longer periods of time.

(b) Carrying out an investigation

This area of learning cannot be differentiated from planning and designing investigations and must be seen as directly connected to the previous area.

Activities should include opportunities to:

- explore materials and living matter eg plants, apparatus available within the classroom situation and school (display, touch and explore areas).

- follow simple instructions with equipment to explore the properties of, effects of, influence of other things on, the equipment. For example:
  (1) seeds can be examined, then placed in different conditions to grow, those that grow can be subjected to further variables by placing them in different positions.
  (2) a piece of material can be examined by feeling it, using a magnifying glass, its properties can be tested for water absorption or elasticity and it could be made into an article of clothing or bag.

- carry out explorations in conjuction with others within the school grounds, local community and on visits to other rural and urban areas. Explorations include naturally occurring situations and those that are set up by an individual, group or class.

- appreciate the need to observe safety rules when carrying out an exploration eg substances should only be tasted with the permission of a known adult.

- **promote the first hand exploration of materials (living and non living) and events.**

- **encourage the sorting, grouping and describing of materials and events in their immediate environment, using their senses and noting similarities and differences.**

- **encourage the use of non standard measures for example, handspans, and the use of standard measures.**

- **introduce the idea of a fair test.**

(c) Recording data

Activities should include opportunities to:

- use stickers or simple marks to record observations on a prepared wall chart or pictogram.

- use a computer/concept keyboard to record and chart observations and results.

- use drawings, models, photographs and video materials for presenting recordings of activites, especially those which have been recorded at a distance from the school or those which change over time.

- use writing, tape recorders, communication with others (verbal/gesture or through dance and drama) to record events.

- set up pictograms, histograms, bar charts, displays etc to show recording in conjunction with others.

- **develop an understanding of the purposes of recording results and so encourage systematic recording, using appropriate methods, including block graphs and frequency charts.**

Many pupils due to physical or sensory impairments will be unable to participate in all the above forms of recording. Some pupils will be dependent on information technology to record as well as to gain access to some areas of scientific work.

The style of recording chosen will need to reflect the ability and age of the pupils. Pupils in key stage 3 and 4 are more likley to be using tape recorders, cameras and videos regularly for recording than those in key stage 1. (See Lawson H. 1992)

Strand (iii) Think and think again – interpret their results and evaluate scientific evidence

Activities should include opportunities to:

- indicate possible interpretations and conclusions in a group situation where an adult helps to facilitate this process by supporting individuals helping to shape their communication into interpretations and conclusions.

- interpret and draw conclusions from their own observations of activities they have been directly involved in. In this way their own ideas and opinions are incorporated into the activity from which conclusions are to be drawn.

- realise that changes and results allow previous actions to be interpreted and conclusions drawn. For example if a greenleafy plant fades in colour when placed in a dark situation and watered but another remains a healthy colour when watered in the light, a conclusion can be drawn that plants like light.

- appreciate the need to test fairly if results are to be interpreted and a true conclusion drawn.

- **encourage the interpretation of results.**

- **encourage pupils to question what they have done and suggest improvements.**

Attainment Target 1: Scientific investigation

Pupils should develop the intellectual and practical skills which will allow them to explore and investigate the world of science and develop a fuller understanding of scientific phenomena, the nature of the theories explaining these and the procedures of scientific investigation. This should take place through activities that require a progressively more systematic and quantified approach which develops and draws upon an increasing knowledge and understanding of science. The activities should encourage the ability to plan and carry out investigations in which pupils:

i)   ask questions, predict and hypothesise;

ii)   observe, measure and manipulate variables;

iii)   interpret their result sand evaluate scientific evidence.

Strand (ii) Observe, measure and manipulate variables

(NB strands (i) and (iii) are not represented at this level)

LEVEL 1 Milestones	STATEMENTS OF ATTAINMENT	EXAMPLE
	Pupils should:	
1 a 1	• react to sensory stimulation (without localising the source).	• respond differentially to small range of smells, tastes, sound inherent in routine events.
1 a 2	• localise source of sensory stimulation; repeat an action which has an interesting environmental effect.	• head turns towards the source of motivating noise near by, touches switch to activate unusual stimulii.
1 a 3	• show interest in/explore some materials and events in their immediate environment.	• touches/looks at twinkling box toy, squeezes, hits, bangs objects together (mouths, touches objects and people for interest, investigation). Moves toys and objects that make a noise (bells, tissue paper may be attached to wrist).
1 a 4	• explore and attend with interest to objects and substances and shift attention from one object/substance to another. Turns, examines object to find appropriate/functional side.	• moves hands in water and sand using more complex actions eg pushing, digging sand, splashing water. Plays with pop up toys, switch toys and equipment eg light, radio. Explores the environment, empties shelves, looks in cupboards (if mobile).
1 a 5	• explore and use with purpose equipment in indoor and outdoor environments. Show interest in events throughout the day, recognising environmental clues in context.	• plays with post box, till, switches, which affect activity taking place. Uses correct side of two sided mirror, uses large brush for brushing leaves outside. Watches animals, leaves, people, traffic etc. Associates noise and smell with lunch time, adult activity and bell with end of session.
1 a 6	• use all their senses to assist their observation of familiar materials and events.	• uses play doh and is aware of the smell and texture (almond essence, lentils, etc introduced to ensure variety). Can associate noise, smell or movement with different animals. Observes the pattern of the school day. Can interpret different sound tapes, recognises familiar smells, identifies objects in a feely bag eg pencil, ball.
1 a	• **observe familiar materials and events.**	• **discuss their ideas while handling and looking at types of sugar crystals and attempting to dissolve them.**

Strand (i) Ask questions, predict and hypothesise

LEVEL 2 Milestones	STATEMENTS OF ATTAINMENT	EXAMPLE
2 a 1	• communicate the desire to know 'why' things happen.	• asks why the snow has melted? Why the flower has died?
2 a 2	• communicate the desire to know 'how' things happen.	• points to newly baked bread and wants to know how it changed shape/rose.
2 a 3	• communicate related responses to questions about 'why' things happen, which show some comprehension of the activity being discussed.	• indicates that the bag broke because it was too full, or the shopping was too heavy.
2 a 4	• communicate related responses to questions about 'how' things happen, which show some comprehension of the activity being discussed.	• communicates that the spring expanded because both ends were pulled.
2 a 5	• communicate the desire to know 'what will happen if'.	• gestures to fish food and communicates what will happen if they are given it all to eat.
2 a 6	• communicate related responses to questions about 'what will happen if', which show comprehension of possible occurrences and activities.	• communicates that the packed lunches must not all be eaten before the woodland walk or they will be very hungry before they get home, perhaps they will not have the energy to finish the walk.
2a	• ask questions such as 'how ...? 'why ...?' and 'what will happen if ...?', suggest ideas and make predictions.	• ask why toy cars go further on a smooth surface than on a rough surface. They could suggest that on very smooth surfaces cars will go faster and further but on a very rough surface they will hardly move at all.

Strand (ii) Observe, measure and manipulate variables

LEVEL 2 Milestones	STATEMENTS OF ATTAINMENT	EXAMPLE
2 b 1	• respond to differences in materials, weather, solutions, routines.	• reacts appropriate to different weather eg puts on coat and hood when going home becuase it is raining, carries coat because it is a hot day.
2 b 2	• sort objects into differing groups based on one set of criteria.	• separates metal and wooden objects.
2 b 3	• sort objects into differing groups according to one criterion of their own choice.	• when presented with a variety of foliage can choose a criterion for sorting eg puts foliage with colourful flowers in one group and the rest in another.

Strand (ii) continued

LEVEL 2 Milestones	STATEMENTS OF ATTAINMENT	EXAMPLE
2 b 5	• identify differences alone or in collaboration with others between different materials, weather, solutions, routines, objects, people.	• in discussion with the class divides the group into those who have straight hair and those who have curly hair.
2b	• **identify simple differences, for example, hot/cold, rough/smooth.**	• **can sort materials into those that feel rough and those that feel smooth.**

Strand (iii) Interpret their results and evaluate scientific evidence

LEVEL 2 Milestones	STATEMENTS OF ATTAINMENT	EXAMPLE
2 e 1	• explore to find out which objects/materials will absorb water and which will not, which float and which sink.	• experiments/plays with sponges, cloth, bricks (plastic and wood) in water.
2 e 2	• explore to find out which objects/materials stretch, bend, tear/snap or change when the temperature alters significantly.	• watch the effect of strong sunlight on a piece of ice, margarine, coloured tissue paper, a leaf.
2 e 3	• explore to find out which objects/materials can be dissolved in water, comparing fairly.	• objects/substances from around the classroom and kitchen area are shaken/stirred in hot and cold water.
2 e 4	• discuss, predict and demonstrate which objects/materials – float sink, dissolve, bend, stretch, tear/snap, change with variation in temperature.	• demonstrates to other pupils a group of materials and objects that have been found in the classroom and can be bent.
2 e 5	• discuss, predict and demonstrate the capacity of objects based on their shape and their ability to change shape by expanding.	• fill balloons, inflatables of different shapes with air or water. Make models with elastic or rubber bands.
2 e 6	• interpret and predict from direct observation or photographs, drawings and models why certain materials were chosen for clothing, building etc.	• look at umbrellas and interpret the materials they are made of must be waterproof.
2 e 7	• interpret findings by associating one factor with another, for example, the pupils' perceptions at this level that 'light objects float', 'thin wood is bendy'.	• can appreciate – thick metal will not bend or break, thick metal is heavy and will sink, polystyrene will break, it is light and will float.
2 e	• **use their observations to support conclusions and compare what they have observed with what they expected.**	• **explain that 'My car went furthest on the hall floor. This is what I thought. Rough carpet slows cars down.'**

Attainment Target 2: Life and living processes

Suggested programme of study leading to the achievement of:
Strand (i) Life processes and the organisation of living things

Level 1

The learning experiences required to achieve the early milestones in this area of learning are closely associated with those suggested for AT 1 in terms of auditory discrimination, visual acuity and kinaesthetic awareness.

Activities should include opportunities to:

- participate in movement sessions in water, in the classroom/hall, assisted by an adult where appropriate.

- participate in relaxation and massage sessions.

- participate in activities where their body movement affects the activity eg painting with body parts, using switch toys or a computer with switches.

- observe, touch, smell, draw and paint plants and other people, being encouraged to note their different parts.

- visit the local community, parks, the open countryside, to observe plants and people.

- use models of plants and people so the different parts can be illustrated by separation and reassembly.

- participate in physical educational activities which assist an awareness of body parts and their names.

- participate in the care and growth of plants being encouraged to indicate when new parts have grown and label them.

- **pupils should find out about themselves and develop their ideas about how they grow, feed, move and use their senses and about the stages of human development.**

AT2 Life and living processes

Strand (i) Life processes and the organisation of living things

LEVEL 1 Milestones	STATEMENTS OF ATTAINMENT	EXAMPLE
1 a 1	• give reflect bodily reactions.	• respond through facial expression or body movement during tactile experiences eg feet in footspar.
1 a 2	• show interest in parts of their body, moving them independently or with assistance.	• look at hands with interest, looks at reflection in mirror. Moves hands/feet when movement reinforced by a reactive environment.
1 a 3	• point to parts of their body when asked.	• follows action communications, plays 'Simon says'.
1 a 4	• show interest in the natural world around them being able to point to a flower, plant, tree or grass when asked.	• looks at, smells flowers etc when taken to local park.
1 a 5	• can point to and label some of their own and their fellow pupils' body parts.	• communicates (labels) head, shoulders, foot etc.
1 a 6	• can find a small variety of leaves, flowers, plants when in a suitable environment.	• participates in a scavenge hunt and finds several items eg root, leaf.
		• draws round fellow pupil naming/signing parts as drawn.
1a	• **be able to name or label the main parts of the human body and a flowering plant.**	• **point to and name observable parts of their bodies, such as knee and elbow, and of a flowering plant such as stem, leaves and petals.**

Attainment Target 2: Life and living processes

Suggested programme of study leading to the achievement of:
Strand (i) Life processes and the organisation of living things

Level 2

Activities should include opportunities to:

- discuss/observe/touch photographs, models and videos that show young and old in plant and animal kingdom.

- observe the changes in plants, animals, babies and themselves as they grow and mature.

- they should be introduced to the main parts of the flowering plants and investigate what plants need to grow and reproduce.

- understanding living things reproduce by observation of their own plant propagation, by visits to farms, observation in the local community and through the use of appropriate photographs, models and video materials.

- look after their personal needs at home and at school as is appropriate to their age.

- enjoy school facilities that allow personal hygiene rules to be followed (eg the provision of water in toilets as well as toilet paper so all pupils can carry out the practice they believe to be the most appropriate).

- utilise role play or dramatic situations to solve problems about what to do if hungry, ill, tired etc.

- look at and recognise medicines and electrical equipment, understanding safety through discussion, video and a respect for safety rules.

- participate in school routines and discuss these with pupils and staff.

- discuss home life, using pictures and stories in conjunction with school activities to follow the pattern of their day.

- pupils should be introduced to ideas about how they keep health through exercise, personal hygiene, diet, rest and personal safety, and to the role of drugs as medicines.

The learning experiences required for a pupil to participate fully in this area of the curriculum should be organised to encourage an awareness of and cooperation with others as well as an understanding of their own needs.

Activities should include opportunities to:

- indicate and meet their own needs in relation to food, drink and rest (encouraging the pupil to make choices and advocate their own needs from an informed basis).

- follow their own daily routine by making diaries that include drawings and photographs of activities. Video recordings could be used to identify different activities that occur throughout the day.

- look after plants and animals in the classroom, in the school and at home, alone and in cooperation with others.

- organise their own clothing to feel comfortable in different weather conditions.

- observe animals in different weather conditions in the local community, on farms as well as on video/film or in pictures commenting on their actions.

- choose where to position a plant and when to water it. To plan the care of an animal.

- over a period, pupils should take responsibility for the care of living things, maintaining their welfare by knowing about their needs and understanding the care required.

When working with plants and animals pupils who have respiratory allergies (asthma/hay fever) or skin allergies may need to be offered alternative suitable activities. Access to plants and animals that do not cause any distress should be offered eg plants with a low pollen yield, scaly animals. (On some occasions staffing adjustments will need to be made if staff have allergies.)

AT2 Life and living processes

Strand (i) Life processes and the organisation of living things

LEVEL 2 Milestones	STATEMENTS OF ATTAINMENT	EXAMPLE
2 a 1	• communicate about source of food or drink, area for rest/sleep and try to obtain desired condition.	• by eye contact, vocalisation, gesture, speech or pulling adult, their desire for a drink, food and sleep.
2 a 2	• know some basic rules of hygiene.	• washes hands before eating meals.
2a	• knows that a person needs to eat, drink and sleep, that animals need to eat, drink and sleep and that plants need water.	• can communicate when tired, hungry, cold etc. Can assist with feeding and cleaning out an animal. Can water plants.
2 a 4	• know that not eating causes hunger, and lack of fluids/drinks causes thirst.	• asks for drink on hot day and can give reason why s/he needs one.
2 a 5	• indicate by action or verbal communication when plants or flowers have died.	• can decide when a plant is dead and requires throwing out, when a plant needs watering, dead leaves removing.
2 a 6	• know to rest or sleep when feeling tired.	• after strenuous activity will sit and rest for a short period, does not object to going to bed when really tired.
2 a 7	• know that in cold weather clothing is different from in hot weather, that some animals change their habits in cold weather.	• can choose appropriate clothing for cold and hot weather, given a choice of clothing.
2 a 8	• know that medicines should be placed out of reach of children and only taken by person they are prescribed for.	• if medicine/syringe found informs adult in charge.
2 a 9	• know simple road safety, not to play with sources of fire, fiddle with electrical equipment.	• looks for pedestrian crossing, if not available uses green cross code.
		• can discuss or indicate appropriate food and drink for plants and animals eg rabbit pellets are not eaten by human beings, human beings eat lettuce but not grass. Can look after nature table removing items that are decaying. Can show understanding of why air is essential to life eg polythene bags are dangerous.
2a	• **know that plants and animals need certain conditions to sustain life.**	• **describe how to look after a pet animal and a potted plant, considering the food, water and environment required.**

Attainment Target 2: Life and living processes

Suggested programme of study leading to the achievement of:

Strand (ii) Variation and the mechanisms of inheritance and evolution

Level 1

The learning experiences required to achieve the early milestones in this area of learning should be controlled to enable a pupil to gradually increase their skills through recognition of and interaction with an ever increasing range of adults and peers.

Activities should include opportunities to:

- establish relationships with the member of staff with whom the pupil is in regular contact with eg class staff, bus escort, lunchtime organiser.

- establish relationships with other pupils in the class group by sharing activities and experiences with them, by being placed in close proximity to them.

- gain experience of a variety of plants and animals by introducing them into the classroom situation to touch and observe.

- observe and interact with adults and children within the whole school through contact during educational activities and at playtime.

- gain experience of plants and animals in the local community through visits to gardens, woodlands, farms and the open countryside.

- develop the recognition of and naming of plants and animals in the classroom and local community.

- they should have opportunities, when possible through first hand observation, to find out about a variety of animal and plant life.

- pupils should consider similarities and differences between themselves and other pupils and understand that individuals are unique.

AT2 Life and living processes

Strand (ii) Variation and the mechanisms of inheritance and evolution

LEVEL 1 Milestones	STATEMENTS OF ATTAINMENT	EXAMPLE
1 a 1	• show recognition by response to main carer.	• changes body movements/behaviour in response to mother, father or main carer.
1 a 2	• respond positively to a significant person, during interaction, needs satisfaction.	• when main carer eg parent is close pupil responds to change in facial expression, body position.
1 a 3	• recognise main carers at home and school, siblings and one or two other pupils.	• shows pleasure, response when main carers, fellow pupils or siblings interact with them.
1 a 4	• respond differentially to several adults and children with whom they are in regular contact.	• when a familiar person interacts with the pupil, ie in the immediate vicinity the pupil responds by change in body position, facial expression, gesture or vocalisation.
1 a 5	• respond to human beings and animals at home, in school and in the local community.	• when human beings or animals are in close proximity produces an obvious response eg touches animals, seeks reaction from adult by eye pointing, vocalisation, movement of self or toy.
1 a 6	• be able to indicate certain human features on self and others.	• move/point to body parts on self and others during activity rhymes and physical education.
1 a 7	• interact with the animal and plant kingdom being able to identify some species from each group.	• participates in group activity eg assembly, observes plants eg smells flowers. Can point to named animals eg cat, dog fish. Can point to sections of the plant kingdom eg tree, bush, flower. • can name verbally or by pointing using living things, pictures, videos and photographs ten animals and ten plants.
1 a 8	• know that age makes a difference to how people look.	• sorts pictures, people according to age eg babies, children and adults. Can indicate/communicate differences, height, hair colour etc.
1 a 9	• know that children often look like their parents because of similar physical features.	• look at family photographs and discuss similar features, ask siblings and parents to school. Look at pictures of identical twins.
1 a 10	• know that people living in different conditions may have some specific features due to environmental conditions.	• discuss what happens to different types of skin in the sun and which is most suited to hot weather.
1 a 11	• know that human beings vary from one individual to the next.	• use language, drawings, photographs and recording to compare how human beings vary in terms of size, skin and hair colour.
1a	• **know that there is a wide variety of living things, which include humans**	• **identify and draw living things they have seen during a walk to school, a visit to a farm or to a park.**

Attainment Target 2:
Life and living processes

Suggested programmes of study leading to the achievement of:

Strand (ii) Variation and the mechanisms of inheritance and evolution

Level 2

The learning experiences required to achieve the early milestones in this area of learning link directly with those in other strands of AT2.

Activities should include opportunities to:

- be involved in school activities where possible with members of the pupil's own family.

- draw, paint, feel, video and photograph themselves and others describing/ indicating similarities and differences.

- be involved in sorting people, models and pictures of people, including family photographs into groups.

- look at photographs, books and videos showing people around the world and in Britain, similarities as well as differences between people being identified, in the context of human understanding and multicultural awareness.

- **they should sort living things into broad groups according to similarities and differences using observable features.**

AT2 Life and living processes

Strand (ii) Variation and the mechanisms of inheritance and evolution

LEVEL 2 Milestones	STATEMENTS OF ATTAINMENT	EXAMPLE
2 a 1	• be able to identify/select an observable feature in familiar living things.	• determine or be assisted to observe a distinct feature eg existence or non existence of eyes, scales, tail, fur, feathers, thorns, leaves.
2 a 2	• be able to sort familiar living things into two groups according to easily observable features.	• plants and animals, furry and feathery creatures.
2 a	• be able to sort familiar living things into broad groups according to easily observable features.	• group animals according to the number of legs or body sections they have, and plants according to leaf shape.

Attainment Target 2:
Life and living processes

Suggested programme of study leading to the achievement of:

Strand (iii) Populations and human influences within ecosystems

Level 2

Activities should include opportunities to:

• explore and identify the main observable features of familiar animals.

• explore and identify observable differences between contrasting areas of the environment to which they can have genuine access.

• experience visits which access specific attention to variations in animals, plants and their environment eg aquarium, park aviaries, park animal corners, farms, greenhouses, bird reserves, garden centre, open country.

• pupils should study plants and animals in a variety of local habitats, for example playing field, garden and pond.

AT 2 Life and living processes

Strand (iii) Populations as human influences within ecosystems

LEVEL 2 Milestones	STATEMENTS OF ATTAINMENT	EXAMPLE
2 a 1	• know of simple differences between birds, fish and mammals.	• communicate that birds have feathers and (generally they) fly, fish have scales and they swim, mammals are furry.
2 a 2	• know of simple differences between land, water and the air above them.	• explore and identify general features of playing fields, ponds.
2 a	• know that different kinds of living things are found in different localities.	• give examples of plants and animals that are found in contrasting areas such as a pond and playing field.

Attainment Target 2: Life and living processes

Suggested programme of study leading to the achievement of:
Strand (iv) Energy and cycles of matter within ecosystems

Level 1

Activities should include opportunities to:

- take responsibility for their own rubbish.

- assist in keeping the school a litter free area, using rubbish containers in the classroom and elsewhere.

- assist in clearing away waste at meal times.

- discuss and make decisions about what should happen to old or discarded items of equipment or furniture.

Level 2

Activities should include opportunities to:

- observe food and natural materials in a variety of situations in school, at shops and in the local neighbourhood, collecting samples. Find different ways to keep food fresh.

- observe man made materials decaying when left in the local environment, or to decay under experimental conditions by the class, or left for prolonged periods of time in an exposed position (eg broken wire fencing).

- discuss the effect pupils and people in the community have on their environment and why this may have changed over recent years (eg take away food with a lot of packaging).

- they should investigate how fast everyday waste products, for example garden refuse, paper, plastic materials and cans decay naturally.

Visits to a tip, refuse disposal unit, recycling plant and collection points or a pig farm that utilises the lunch waste are all useful and stimulating activities when working this area. A link with world resources falls naturally into this work, linking this attainment target with geography. At an early stage observation of the refuse collection truck is possible, a note being made of when it comes and the activities of the refuse collectors.

AT 2 Life and living processes

Strand (iv) Energy and cycles of matter within ecosystems

LEVEL 1 Milestones	STATEMENTS OF ATTAINMENT	EXAMPLE
1 a 3	• know that rubbish is thrown away in certain places.	• place paper towel in bin. Place classroom waste in bin provided.
1 a 4	• know that small rubbish bins are emptied into larger containers.	• empties class rubbish into outside bin container.
1 a 5	• know that toys, cars, furniture that is broken beyond repair is rubbish, know that packaging round food is rubbish, know that food left on a plate when a meal is finished is waste.	• helps to place discarded large items eg broken chair in general rubbish area or helps burn, take to tip. Place crisp packet or bun case in rubbish bin.
1 a 6	• know that in the preparation of some food there are waste products, know that when gardening some rubbish will be collected and placed in an appropriate place.	• throws orange peel, banana skin, vegetable peel away when preparing simple food. Places leaves and grass cuttings on compost, paper and tin cans in rubbish bin.
1 a	**• know that human activities produce a wide range of waste products.**	**• assists in removing rubbish after events eg school fair, party, disco.**

LEVEL 2 Milestones		
2 a 2	• know that some waste products they observe are beginning to decay.	• can observe and identify evidence of decay eg fruit that if over ripe/damaged, rust on metal, paper disintegrating.
2 a 4	• know which waste products will decay quickly and which will take a long time.	• can sort vegetation eg fruit, vegetables and small plants into a group that will decay readily, paper and cardboard into another group that may take longer to decay and metal and polythene objects inot a group that will take a very long time to decay.
2 a	**• know that some waste products decay naturally, but do so over different periods of time.**	**• describe the changes that occur in items such as fruit, a newspaper, a tin can and a plastic bottle, when buried in soil for several weeks.**

Attainment Target 3: Materials and their properties

Suggested programme of study leading to the achievement of:

Strand (i) The properties, classification and structure of materials

Level 1

The learning experiences required to achieve the early milestones in this area of learning are closely associated with those suggested for Sc1 in the area of kinaesthetic awareness.

Activities should include opportunities to:

- experience feeling/manipulating toys/objects which give interesting feedback being made of a variety of materials and of different shapes and sizes.

- experience feeling/manipulating solid and liquid materials, natural and manufactured with time being given to express responses.

- experience materials that change in shape, consistency eg in cookery, the sand pit, water play (ice introduced into water etc), use of malleable creative materials eg clay.

- participate in a school/classroom environment where natural and manufactured materials are available to explore freely.

- experience change in materials through the use of tools eg simple woodwork and metalwork (link with technology).

- participate in outdoor activities when materials may be made to change shape and form eg digging on beaches, sea and sand mixing, piling leaves up and squashing them.

- **pupils should collect and find similarities and differences between a variety of everyday materials.**

Some of the materials available for exploration should be changed regularly to assist the pupil's desire to touch and look on a daily basis. Pupils who are unable to explore independently should be assisted by an adult who endeavours to be sensitive to their communications about the exploration.

AT 3 Materials and their properties

Strand (i) The properties, classification and structure of materials

LEVEL 1 Milestones	STATEMENTS OF ATTAINMENT	EXAMPLE
1 a 1	• react to visual and tactile stimulation without localising the source.	• changes behaviour in response to tactile stimulation, eg warmth of human body when held, body contact with hard and soft surfaces, warm and cool surfaces.
1 a 2	• localise source of visual or tactile stimulation.	• orientates head/eyes towards source of light, positions body to avoid or increase, disliked/liked tactile stimulation.
1 a 3	• show interest in materials/objects that change in shape.	• moves part of body in sand, play doe, handcream, paint.
1 a 4	• discriminate between toys/objects to play with, being attracted by shape, colour, flexibility or texture.	• chooses specific toys/objects being attracted by their properties eg small or warm to hold, visually attractive – bright or reflective colours.
1 a 5	• communicate about specific aspects of objects/toys, for example colour, shape or texture.	• vocalises or indicates specific aspects of objects/toys that are of interest eg takes bendy toy animal to show an adult, demonstrates the flexibility.
1 a 6	• describe two properties of an object. Communicate if the object can change in shape.	• describes verbally or by gesture properties relating to shape, colour and texture. Can show how objects can be affected by squashing, spreading and squeezing.
1 a	• **be able to describe the simple properties of familiar materials.**	• **describe aluminium foil as shiny and hard, damp sand as gritty and wet, and wool as soft and light.**

Attainment Target 3: Materials and their properties

Suggested programme of study leading to the achievement of:
Strand (i) The properties, classification and structure of materials

Level 2

Activities should include opportunities to:

- freely explore materials naturally occurring in the classroom as well as those specifically introduced to encourage investigation. The provision of an area where all members of the class can bring a range of materials for investigation is useful, as is the opportunity for groups to go out collecting and 'scavenging' in the local area and beyond.

- explore materials to find out their properties:
  - choose materials to see which will dissolve in different liquids (flour, sand, iron filings, salt in water, oil, milk).
  - choose materials to see which are rigid and which flexible.
  - choose materials to see which are transparent and which are opaque.
  - choose materials to see which are reflective and which are non reflective (shiny and dull materials can be incorporated into this area).

The materials should be touched, rubbed, stretched, twisted, squeezed, torn, squashed, bent, poured, subjected to temperature changes, mixed together as much as possible. Pupils should be encouraged to investigate through their own ideas. Some pupils will need staff support during some of this investigation.

- **these should include natural and manufactured materials such as rocks, soil, air, water and other liquids, cooking ingredients and metallic objects.**

- **they should explore the properties of these materials referring for example to their *shape, colour and texture* and consider some of their everyday uses.**

AT 3 Materials and their properties

Strand (i) The properties, classification and structure of materials

LEVEL 2 Milestones	STATEMENTS OF ATTAINMENT	EXAMPLE
2 a 1	• be able to recognise a difference or similarity between two materials.	• when given a material can find a similar one from a selection on the table eg margarine and Vaseline, both can be spread, both change shape easily.
2 b 1	• be able to sort materials into two groups according to one characteristic.	• group stones, matals, fabrics, wool and wood according to their properties of hard and soft.
2 a 2	• be able to recognise/find out which materials are transparent and which are not, which materials are reflective/shiny or dull.	• investigate objects in the classroom, which can be seen through, which can you see yourself in.
2 b 2	• be able to divide materials into two groups according to two characteristics.	• group wool, glass, string, bricks, spanner, fork, towel according to their properties of hard/rigid and soft/flexible.
2 a 3	• be able to recognise/find out which materials are hard or soft, flexible or rigid.	• feel materials in a feely bag, find two that feel flexible eg rubber and pipe cleaner.
		• find materials in the classroom that have similarities or differences eg coin and scissors, both are cold to touch and rigid, water and pencil, one can continually change shape the other is a static shape, one transparent the other opaque.
2 b 3	• be able to group materials into two groups according to characteristics of their own choosing.	• collect materials from the school building and grounds and group them according to their properties eg glass, mirror, tin foil, – reflective and hard, toilet paper, jumper, sponge ball – soft and opaque.
2 a/b	• **be able to group materials according to observable features.**	• **sort and group materials according to their shape, colour of hardness.**

Attainment Target 3:
Materials and their properties

Suggested programme of study leading to the achievement of:
Strand (iii) Chemical changes

Level 2

Activities should include opportunities to:

- produce new objects from a variety of materials:

    - using different basic ingredients make items of food eg flour plus water plus small amounts of other ingredients makes a wide range of staple foods – chappati, roti, bread (variety of types), nan, poppadom etc.
    - using different substances make a variety of paints eg powder paint mixed with different amounts of water or washing up liquid. Using old materials including paper attempt to make recycled paper (cross ref PoS Sc 2 strand (iv)).

They should expore the effects of heating some everyday substances for example *ice, water, wax and chocolate*, in order to understand how heating and cooling bring about melting and solidifying.

They should observe materials such as dough, wood and clay which change permanently on heating.

Throughout this work pupils must be given the opportunity to compare and contrast within the practical situation. Pupils must be given the opportunity to instigate their own investigation of materials and objects, bringing in objects and materials from outside the school. Materials must always be associated with real objects for example – glass of varying colour/thickness associated with windows, glasses, vases, fabric associated with clothing, soft furnishings.

AT3 Materials and their properties

Strand (iii) Chemical changes

LEVEL 2 Milestones	STATEMENTS OF ATTAINMENT	EXAMPLE
2 c 1	• know that water changes to ice when cooled/ frozen and to steam when heated/boiled.	• place water in the freezer compartment of a fridge and watch how it freezes over time. Watch water steam as it is heated.
2 c 3	• know that when ingredients are mixed for baking and cooked they form a new material.	• watch margarine change from a solid to a liquid as it is melted to make biscuits, add other ingredients and a soft solid appears, on cooking a hard biscuit is produced.
		• watch the effects of weather on the environment and materials in the home or school eg puddles turn to ice in the cold, dry up in the sun, chocolate biscuits melt on a hot day, the milk freezes and pushes the top off a bottle on a cold day.
2 c	• **know that heating and cooling everyday materials can cause them to melt or solidify or change permanently.**	• **describe the formation and melting of ice and a cake mixture before and after baking.**

Attainment Target 4:
Physical processes

Suggested programme of study leading to the achievement of:
Strand (i) Electricity and magnetism

Level 1

Activities should include opportunities to:

- experience sensitive multi sensory activities, whereby reflex movements are given appropriate and interesting feedback. A variety of adapted switches eg tilt, beam, slide, pressure, micropone, two hand switches which can be activated by any part of the body, should be available.

- participate in observation of, and safe play and experimentation with, devices which require a source of electrical power, in order to make them work. Battery operated appliances should precede those requiring mains electricity.

- observe that some appliances need connecting to an electrical power source (need plugging in), in order to operate them.

- observe and use appropriate electrical appliances, under close supervision of an adult, responding to basic safety instructions and warnings as directed.

- experience using a variety of battery or mains electric powered toys, games and age appropriate electrical equipment, responding to any safety instructions and precautions as directed by a nearby adult.

- experience practical activities with toys, games and everyday age appropriate electrical equipment in functional contexts such as boiling a kettle to make hot drinks, using a hair drier to dry hair after washing, operating a cassette recorder to listen to music, using an iron following laundry of clothes. Pupils should spontaneously adopt safety precautions and avoid dangers, either as an acquired learnt behaviour, or because their knowledge helps them know the potential dangers if safety rules are not followed.

- **pupils should be made aware of some of the uses of electricity in the classroom and in the home and the dangers of misuse.**

AT 4 Physical processes

Strand (i) Electricity and magnetism

LEVEL 1 Milestones	STATEMENTS OF ATTAINMENT	EXAMPLE
1 a 1	• make reflect movements for which motivating sensory feedback is given, using an appropriate switch	• make random movements which affect pressure or tilt switch, to activate visual, auditory, vibratory stimulation as appropriate.
1 a 2	• intentionally and consistently use a variety of switches so as to activate battery operated pieces of equipment	• use tilt switch operated by deliberate head or leg movement in order to activate use, vibrating platform, tape recorder or a pressure switch operated by eg whole body movement or hand to activate visually stimulating computer programmes, musical toys and equipment.
1 a 4	• know that a variety of household/school appliances and toys use batteries in order to make them work.	• exploration of appliances and toys such as torches, clocks, battery operated lego kits, musical toys, personal cassette.
1 a 5	• know that some household/school appliances need a plug to connect them to an electrical power source ie a socket, in order to make them work.	• is aware that some devices need 'plugging in', and will wait for or request another person to do so, such as a tape recorder, TV, radio, toaster, hoover.
1 a 6	• respond to appropriate safety precautions when near to or operating any form of electrical appliance.	• obeys instructions given by adult related to common dangers and safety eg 'No', 'Stop', 'Don't touch', 'Dry your hands'.
		• aware of a wider range of electrically operated appliances eg computer, washing machine, refrigerator. Knows metal items other than electrical plugs should not be inserted into a socket.
1 a	• **know that many household appliances use electricity but that misuse is dangerous.**	• **name electrical appliances in their home and talk about some of the dangers associated with them.**

Attainment Target 4:
Physical processes

Suggested programme of study leading to the achievement of:
Strand (i) Electricity and magnetism

Level 2

Activities should include opportunities to:

- experience manipulating magnets of all shapes and sizes eg horseshoe, bar, cylindrical and button magnets.

- experiment with magnets in the classroom, discovering any magnetic reaction to eg door handles, pipes, keys, taps, tools, radiators, chains, window frames.

- experiment with magnets and everyday classroom materials, discovering differences in magnetic reaction to eg pencils, lego, paper clips, cutlery, coins, pins, scissors.

- use magnets to sort between two sets or mixed collections of items, into those which are attracted by magnets and those which are not eg shells and washers, iron and brass filings, steel and plastic buttons, iron and brass screws.

- extend their practise with magnetic materials, through the medium of play and games, such as magnetic boards/shapes/letters/numbers, magnetic fishing game, games in which items can be moved by dragging magnets underneath surface. Use magnet to pick up pins from tray of sawdust. Experimentation with magnet and needle suspended on thread, magnet and compass needle. Stroking materials made of iron to magnetise them. Magnetism through water and different materials and surfaces.

- explore that magnets repel each other, such as, placing round pot magnets on a wooden rod in different orders, finding which end of a magnet can hold the longest 'necklace' of small nails.

- **they should explore the effect of magnets on a variety of magnetic and non magnetic materials and consider their uses.**

AT 4 Physical processes

Strand (i) Electricity and magnetism

LEVEL 2 Milestones	STATEMENTS OF ATTAINMENT	EXAMPLE
2 a 1	• be able to use a magnet to sort items into those which are attracted by magnets, and those which are not.	• mixed collections which include items which are made of steel, and those with no steal component, such as steel and brass washers, iron and brass filings, steel, brass and plastic buttons, steel and plastic paper clips.
2 a 4	• be able to demonstrate that magnets can repel each other.	• exploration of bar magnets, placing them in different positions to experience, attract and repel action, according to proximity of like and unlike poles. • experience using a variety of magnets of different shapes, sizes and strengths to find out about how they affect each other and other materials. Games which encourage observations related to magnetism eg magnetic fishing game.
2 a	• know that magnets attract some materials but not others and can repel each other.	• show how a magnet can be used as a means to sort objects and how repulsion between two magnets can be used to propel a simple toy vehicle.

AT 4 Physical processes

Suggested programme of study leading to the achievement of:
Strand (ii) Energy resources and energy transfer
Level 2

Activities should include opportunities to:

- explore ways of adjusting their circumstances according to personal feelings related to body temperature, as in addition or removal of clothing, position of self in relation to indoor and outdoor temperatures.

- explore differences in temperature in everyday contexts as in recognition of the hot and cold water taps, preparation of washing up and bath water, preparation of hot and cold food and drinks.

- observe the effects of heating and cooling on substances as in food preparation and simple experiments eg freezing and melting water/ice, lighted candle.

- **they should talk about when and why they feel hot or cold and link the sensations of hot and cold with thermometer measurements for example in *water and air.***

LEVEL 2 Milestones	STATEMENTS OF ATTAINMENT	EXAMPLE
2 b 1	• be able to communicate the need to have adjusted, or independently adjust their own clothing according to personal comfort, regarding own body temperature.	• remove coat or jumper when hot. Put on extra clothing when cold.
2 b 3	• be able to take appropriate actions to accommodate personal requirements related to own body temperature.	• request or help self to cold drinks in hot weather. Move near to or away from fire/radiator according to room temperature.
		• experience and indicate feelings related to own body temperature in different contexts. Effects of clothing, weather conditions, diet, room temperature. Changes in feelings eg coming from cold outdoors to warmth indoors.
2 b	• **understand the meaning of hot and cold relative to the temperature of their own bodies.**	• **determine whether hot and cold tap water are warmer or cooler than themselves by feeling them and using a thermometer.**

Attainment Target 4: Physical processes

Suggested programme of study leading to the achievement of:
Strand (iii) Forces and their effects

Level 1

Activities should include opportunities to:

- participate in a few selected physical push and pull movements eg being rocked, patted, turned, rolled, in safe comfortable contexts, with a reassuring adult.

- experience and react to different types of sensitively created physical bodily movements, which incorporate push and pull, slow and fast, jerky and smooth, starting and stopping, swinging and turning actions, in pleasurable contexts.

- experience and react to being pushed and pulled in trolley, wheelchair, gokart, on swings etc.

- use pushing actions upon small and large toys and equipment, which lend themselves to being pushed.

- explore the effects of pushes on things using any part of the body to create the action.

- actively engage in play which encourages moving and operating a wide range of small and large apparatus and toys, both indoors and outdoors.

- demonstrate in naturally occurring and devised situational contexts, how items can be moved.

- **pupils should have early experience of devices which move.**

NOTE: Pupils with physical disabilities should be assisted to participate as fully as possible in push and pull activities, by adapting equipment where necessary, and through other staff and pupils cooperating with them.

AT 4 Physical processes

Strand (iii) Forces and their effects

LEVEL 1 Milestones	STATEMENTS OF ATTAINMENT	EXAMPLE
1 b 1	• be able to make random reflex responses to materials providing sensory stimulation.	• changes body movement, hand/finger/ mouth movement.
1 b 2	• react by repetition of simple action to recreate interesting effect.	• hits/swipes/kicks motivating objects/dangling toys, thus creating interesting movement. Pulls/cloth off face/legs in play. Pushes/ kicks floats/inflatables in hydrotherapy pool.
1 b 3	• be able to cause movement in a variety of small and large items of equipment/toys which lend themselves to being pushed and pulled.	• pushes and pulls large equipment eg walking frame, swing, wheelbarrow. Pushes and pulls small equipment eg toy cars, marbles. Pushes and pulls doors/cupboards open and shut.
1 b 4	• be able to cause movement, using a pushing or pulling action in a variety of ways using different parts of the body.	• pushing movements involved in kicking/rolling ball, hockey. Pushing floats in swimming pool with hands/feet. Pushing/pulling totally soft play equipment with any part of body. Pushing on pedals to move bicycle.

• demonstrates an understanding of the principle by taking appropriate action in context ie pushes/pulls items in order to move them such as PE apparatus, outdoor play equipment, a supermarket trolley, a wheelbarrow, gates, furniture, trolley. |
| 1 b | • understanding that things can be moved by pushing or pulling them. | • using a range of toys that move, show how pushes or pulls are needed to get them moving. |

Page 58

Attainment Target 4:
Physical processes

Suggested programme of study leading to the achievement of:
Strand (iii) Forces and their effects

Level 2

Activities should include opportunities to:

- explore the use of pushes and pulls to perform own body movements eg water confidence activities, swimming, jumping, trampolining, climbing.

- explore the effects of pushes and pulls in cooperative contexts with a partner eg action songs, PE, joint movement of furniture.

- explore and compare the effects of pushes and pulls on a variety of small and large items and equipment, in different contexts eg on tarmac or grass, up or down slopes.

- explore ways of moving items, involving them in problem solving situations eg heavy items might be moved on a trolley, in a wheelbarrow. Several people make pushing of Canadian canoe from land to water easier.

- visit places of interest, where demonstration of the actions of pushes and pulls can be observed eg museum of science and technology, factories, building site.

- experience the effects of pushes and pulls on a variety of movements and speed, through having opportunities to engage in first hand practise in operating equipment eg trucks, tricycles, bicycles, scooter, hoover.

- and manufactured forces such as those produced by wind up toys, elastic or electrically driven toys.

- and by the movement of their bodies.

- these forces should be experienced in the way they push, pull, make things move, stop things and change the shape of objects. Such experiences could include, for example, *road safety activities*.

- **pupils should have early experience of devices which move.**

AT 4 Physical processes

Strand (iii) Forces and their effects

LEVEL 2 Milestones	STATEMENTS OF ATTAINMENT	EXAMPLE
2 c 1	• be able to cause movement in a variety of large and small equipment using a pushing or pulling action, or a combination of both.	• effects of pushing and pulling activities on a partner in PE. Opening and closing of drawers, cupboards, doors, gates. Investigation of springs.
2 c 3	• be able to demonstrate the variations in speed of items, according to the force exerted by push and pull actions.	• comparison of gentle and strong push and/ or pull action on balls, balloon on string, toy cars, trucks, boxes on wheels, marbles.
		• demonstrate skills involved when riding tri-cycle/bicycle: operating pedals, brakes, changing speed, swerving, turning and stopping. Paddling a canoe. Hoovering a carpet avoiding obstacles.
2 c	• understand that pushes and pulls can make things start moving, speed up, slow down or stop.	• show and explain, using moving toys, how pushes and pulls can start or stop motion and also affect how fast things move.

Attainment Target 4: Physical processes

Suggested programme of study leading to the achievement of:
Strand (iv) Light and sound

Level 1

The learning experiences required to achieve the early milestones are closely associated with those sugested for AT 1, in terms of sight and visual acuity.

Activities should include opportunities to:

- observe and follow movement of lights/colours eg torch, shiny paper, using eyes and movement of head. Reaching to touch source of light/colour. Using any part of the body to operate switches eg pressure pad, tilt switch, to create or change light and/or colour.

- participate in sensory experience which promote observation/fascination with colours. At an early level, attention to colour may be reinforced by accompanying sound reinforcement.

- experience and explore a range of sounds which can be made orally and through a variety of actions on different parts of the body.

- observe daytime and nighttime sources of light. Access to observation of night-time sources of light should be incorporated through the use of video, slides, pictures, visits eg planetarium, and where possible through first hand experiences.

- make choices according to colour, in order to draw attention to the colour factor eg clothing, food and drinks, toys, water play/bubble bath colours, expansive creative mediums.

- participate in the exploration of a range of sounds which can be created using everyday objects, and a range of simple to handle musical instruments.

- observe and investigate a range of light sources. Pupils should have access to safe equipment/items from which light can be observed/created eg torches, lamps, mirrors, glass, plastic, A/V aids, shiny materials, dimmer switches.

- match and sort a variety of natural and manufactured items according to their colours.

- listen to and identify sounds which occur in everyday indoor and outdoor situations. Variety of household, classroom and environmental sounds.

- observe, under guidance of an adult, sources of light eg from a candle, a match, fires, electrical light sources, traffic lights.

- explore and observe the use of colour in everday contexts eg people's hair, eyes, clothing, PE kit, plates, cups. Colours in the classroom, including specific colour areas. Colours of food, cars, playground apparatus.

- match taped sounds to real sounds. Use a tape recorder in the context of games to listen to and record a variety of sounds eg making some kitchen, animal, noisy or soft sounds, and sound lotto type games.

- observe variations in light indoors and outdoors, by experiencing contrasting light, shady and dark environments/contexts. This may occur through the following learning opportunities: the use of coloured lighting/spotlights in dance/drama, photography, sitting in a darkened room to view TV/video. The opportunity to experience light variation: in PE indoor and outdoor activities through the use of barrels, boxes, parachutes or during activities eg a walk in the woods, caving, camping, in play and the creation of 'dens'.

- observe colours in the environment, including those which remain static and those which change eg natural environmental colours, colours in the shops, the streets, of traffic,buildings. Observation of colour changes by looking through coloured mediums eg cellophane, coloured glasses, coloured water, material.

- explore and demonstrate variations in the volume of sounds.

- experience visits which access attention to variations in light eg mining museum, mosque, church, aquarium.

- observe and experiment with the different effects of colour eg face painting, make up, clothing, table settings, arranging flowers, the nature table, cooking and meal arrangement, creative activities.

- explore sounds seeking their source.

Pupils should be able to participate in a range of multicultural events, workshops and concerts which stimulate and broaden their knowledge of the rich and wide ranging cultural sounds, instruments and music which exist. Attention to sounds may be further explored across the whole curriculum eg going out on a listening walk, communicating about which sounds are heard and where they may have come from. Stories and puppet play may be accompanied by sound effects. Individual and cooperative responses to sounds in dance. Classification activities eg liked/disliked, soft/loud, long/short, high/low sounds.

- **pupils should have opportunities to explore light sources and the effects related to shadow, reflection and colour.**

- **pupils should have the opportunity to experience the range of sounds in their immediate environment, and to find out about their causes and uses.**

- **they should explore how to make and experience sounds by speaking and singing, striking, plucking, shaking, scraping and blowing, using *familiar objects and simple musical instruments from a variety of cultural traditions*.**

AT 4 Physical processes

Strand (iv) Light and sound

LEVEL 1 Milestones	STATEMENTS OF ATTAINMENT	EXAMPLE
1 c 1	• react to changes from light to dark.	• changes body movement in response to light/dark.
	• respond to clear bright colours.	• light stimulation eg responses such as fleeting eye contact, any body movement, to different coloured contrasting lights et blue and yellow.
	• respond differentially to a range of sounds.	• change in voice/body movement/facial expression, 'stilling', eye contact at familiar voice/sounds. Startle reflex/stiffening at unfamiliar loud sounds.
1 c 2	• locate, fixate and follow visual image/light source in all directions.	• will look towards and follow movement of adult eye contact, bright objects, lights, using eyes and body orientation. Reaches out to touch source of light.
	• respond differentially to contrasting colours, or favourite items according to colour given a choice.	• gives stronger eye contact/body orientation/ reaching behaviour to some colours as opposed to others.
1 c 3	• locate, fixate or turn towards sources of sounds.	• orientate body/face/eyes/arms towards motivating environmental sound/voice.
	• know which are the usual daytime and nighttime sources of light.	• can associate daytime with a light sky, the sun, less need for artificial lighting. Can associate night-time with a dark sky, the moon, stars, more need for artificial lighting.
	• be able to match colours.	• colour match using object to object and object to picture.
	• be able to produce a range of sound using their own body.	• oral sounds eg blowing, vocalisations, singing. Sounds using different actions and different parts of the body eg clapping hands, tapping, stamping, patting chest, sides, knees.
1 c 4	• be able to recognise some differences between light, dark and shade, in natural environments and through created atmospheres.	• make rooms lighter/darker by switching lights on/off, opening/drawing curtains or blinds. Experiences of different shades of light eg under tunnels, bridges, amongst trees, in cave, under parachute or inside tunnel in PE.
	• be able to sort by colour, natural and manufactured items.	• sort by colour classroom materials: beads, crayons, bricks. Miscellaneous materials: buttons, cups, clothing. Natural materials: fir cones, leaves, vegetables.

Strand (iv) continued

LEVEL 1 Milestones	STATEMENTS OF ATTAINMENT	EXAMPLE
1 c 5	• know that light comes from different sources.	• natural: sun, moon, stars. Artificial: light bulbs, neon lights, television, torch, car head-lamps. Light radiated by heat: candle. Reflected light: from a mirror, tin foil, metal.
	• know of the usual colours of a few items.	• obvious associations eg colours of fruits: banana/yellow, orange/orange; vegetables: peas/green, carrots/orange; outdoors: sun/yellow, grass/green.
	• be able to recognise a few natural, household or street sounds.	• wind, rain, birds, animals or rustling leaves. A running tap, the kettle, the door or the TV. Traffic noises, aeroplanes, sirens, industrial noises or footsteps.
1 c	• **know about the simple properties of sound and light.**	• **make a variety of sound from soft to loud using a range of objects; explain that light comes from many sources and can be of different colours.**

Attainment Target 4: Physical processes

Suggested programme of study leading to the achievement of:
Strand (iv) Light and sound

Level 2

Activities should include opportunities to:

- observe unusual everyday materials through which light can pass eg windows, clear water.

- observe and experiment with the effects of a range of sources of light to discover their effects upon transparent, translucent and opaque materials.

- understand what shadows are, through simple activities and games which draw attention to them eg making and using shadow puppets, making hand shapes on a projector screen, making own shadows fat, long, small, jumping on each others' shadows, drawing round shadows of objects.

- participate in drawing and picture making activities which encourage confidence and experimentation in representing abstract and representational images, using 2D and 3D mediums.

- observe the existence of and changes in colour, light and shade in everday indoor and outdoor contexts.

- observe, participate and experiment in changing and using shades of colour to bring about original and desired effects.

- observe and experiment with the effects of light, colour and shade using audio/visual aids eg photographic mediums, computer designs.

- **pupils should have opportunities to explore light sources and the effects related to shadow, reflection and colour.**

AT 4 Physical processes

Strand (iv) Light and sound

LEVEL 2 Milestones	STATEMENTS OF ATTAINMENT	EXAMPLE
2 d 1	• know of a few materials through which light can pass.	• comparison of light variation between plain window, and window with blinds/curtains drawn across. Comparison between materials: those we can see through, those we can't, eg cling film, polythene, glass bottles, wood, bricks, pot, water.
2 d 3	• be able to identify shadows in any circumstance.	• own shadows in sunlight. Shadows in areas of classroom. Shadows in playground. Shadows in the wider environment of trees, buildings.
2 d	• **know that light passes through some materials and that when it does not, shadows may be formed.**	• **explain that a light source needs to be blocked in a controlled way for finger shadows to be made.**

Attainment Target 4:
Physical processes

Suggested programme of study leading to the achievement of:
Strand (iv) The Earth's place in the Universe

Level 1

Activities should include opportunities to:

•   observe and communicate about the features of different skies.

•   communicate about factors related to the sun such as its appearance and disappearance: the existence of shady and sunlit areas and factors related to the apparent changes in the position of the sun.

•   **they should observe, over a period of time, the length of daylight, the position of the sun, and when possible the position of the moon in the sky and its changing appearance.**

AT 4 Physical processes

Strand (v) The Earth's place in the Universe

LEVEL 1 Milestones	STATEMENTS OF ATTAINMENT	EXAMPLE
1d3	• be able to indicate or name any features related to a day or night sky.	• communicate about features such as the sun, moon, clouds, stars in relation to real sky, or skies in photographs, video. Draws attention to things which move across the sky, clouds on breezy days, birds, aeroplanes.
1d4	• know that the sun appears and disappears.	• observes and communicates about sunrise/appearance of the sun in the day, sunset/disappearance of sun at night. Appearance and disappearance of sun when cloudy. The fact that the sun can be obscured by trees, landscape, buildings.
1d5	• be able to discriminate between sunlit and non sunlit areas.	• observes and communicates that parts of classroom, school building, playground, or other indoor or outdoor areas, are in sunlight or in shade.

Strand (v) continued

LEVEL 1 Milestones	STATEMENTS OF ATTAINMENT	EXAMPLE
1 d 6	• know that the sun changes position in the sky.	• observes and communicates that the sun shines through different classroom/school windows, or on different areas of the school building/playground, own home/garden, as the day progresses. • observes and communicates about general patterns of apparent movement of the sun. Knows that the sun rise (goes up), goes high in the sky, and then sets (goes down).
1 d	• **be able to describe the apparent movement of the sun across the sky.**	• **note the position of the sun through the same window in the classroom at different times of the day and draw picture showing its position.**

Level 2

Activities should include opportunities to:

- communicate about usual changes which occur between daytime and night-time.

- participate in simple practical demonstrations of the principle as to why night occurs eg using a torch to represent the sun and an orange to represent the Earth. Mark the orange with a spot representing hometown, then shining the torch on the dot rotate the orange slowly to represent the movement of the Earth in relation to the sun, and observe the changes in light and dark on the area of the dot.

- associate routines and factors related to daytime and nighttime, in order to understand when one begins and one ends and acknowledge that it may be dark or light at bedtime/breakfast time according to different times of the year.

- participate in recording variations in day length using graphs and charts. Winter would be the most accessible period to monitor closely within the school context.

- identify spherical shapes, and accept/associate these with the shape of the Earth.

- observe the shape of the Earth, using a globe and through audio/visual aids. Relate places on a map to places on a globe.

- associate Earth as the planet populated by people.

- explore the fact that the Earth, moon and sun are separate bodies, using practical 3D models, and through access to audio visual materials as aids.

- observe and discover factors related to the Earth and other planets, through visits to places which assist in this understanding eg a planetarium, science and technology museum.

- **they should observe, over a period of time, the length of daylight, the position of the sun, and when possible the position of the moon in the sky and its changing appearance.**

AT4 Physical processes

Strand (v) The Earth's place in the Universe

LEVEL 2 Milestones	STATEMENTS OF ATTAINMENT	EXAMPLE
2 e 1	• be able to identify the Earth, moon and sun, in a 3D model of the solar system.	• identify a globe as representing the Earth. Recognise, point to, name or discuss the individual planets, in a representational model.
2 e 2	• be able to identify the Earth, moon and sun, in 2D representations of the solar system.	• recognise, point to, name or discuss the individual planets in pictures and related slides and video materials.
		• demonstrate that movement of planets is only possible, because they are separate bodies. Know that men/women need to travel in order to reach the moon.
2e	• **know that the Earth, sun and moon are separate spherical bodies.**	• **be asked to imagine they are on a spacecraft looking out of the windows and draw the Earth, sun and moon as they would see them from space.**

Recording and Assessment

'There are two main aspects to record keeping; logging the work done and recording the individual child's achievements. The record of the work done will ensure that teachers can monitor the breadth, balance and relevance of the planned activities.'

Science non-statutory orders NCC 1989.

'Teacher assessment is part of everyday classroom activity, designed to find out what individual children know, understand and can do and to assist in the planning of future work. It is a continuous process rather than a separate activity necessarily requiring the use of extra tasks or tests.'

Science Non-Statutory Guidance (1991).

Class and individual records play a vital role in ensuring that each pupil receives a science curriculum which has breadth and progression through their school career. Many pupils with severe and complex learning difficulties attend the same school throughout their school life. Such an all age school has a responsiblity to deliver a curriculum that is age appropriate. The school curriculum which will now incorporate the National Curriculum provides a structure on which the staff, parents and governors of a school can base their recording system. Figure 3 illustrates an easy method of recording topics which can help to ensure excessive repetition of aspects of the science curriculum does not occur.

Ongoing techer assessment plays a vital role for all pupils and for pupils with severe and complex learning difficulties this assessment may be even more crucial. Although it is the intention of SEAC to assess pupils with special needs using SATs (SEAC 1989) this may well not prove a possible task. Legislation allows the disapplication of SATs for individual pupils for whom they are deemed as totally inappropriate by their school and teaching staff. For pupils who do not participate in SATs teacher assessment will stand alone. The milestones steps that are presented in this document relating to each attainment target could offer a useful basis for teacher assessment. Figure 4 illustrates how one of the statements of attainment in attainment target 1 might be assessed. For many pupils the milestone steps will require further individual breakdown allowing for more detailed assessment and thus enhancing pupil progress. For a few pupils the statements of attainment alone may be sufficient for recording.

Recording of a pupil's work could include:

- written notes relating to the topic/module and the individual's response to the work.

- a checklist showing which attainment targets have been covered.

- videos demonstrating the pupil's activities.

A record of achievements file for each pupil could include:

- photographs of the individual engaged in activities.

- records of their achievements.

- examples of their work.

Such a document has relevance for the pupil, their family and all those who continue the development of the pupil's scientific skills.

Models for Assessment and Recording

Figures 3 and 4 illustrate models of recording and assessment that assist the teacher to plan future learning, the pupil's progress over the past few years being seen at a glance. Note is made of the areas of learning a pupil has participated in and reacted to – **experienced** (E). Pupils who have been working towards a milestone but not managed to achieve that level of learning consistently are recorded as **studying** (S) that area implying some further work would lead to **achievement** (A). Staff may need to personalise the milestone steps for each pupil for example through task analysis.

Other validated assessments will also assist the teacher in this curricular area. This is particularly true when assessing pupils with profound and multiple learning difficulties. The Behaviour Assessment Battery (Kiernan and Jones 1982) and The Next Step to the Ladder (Simon 1987) are both valuable.

The process of recording and assessment may in the long term highlight areas in which additional resources are required.

A Framework for Recording Topic Titles

TOPICS COVERED:					
Year	Year Group	AUTUMN	SPRING	SUMMER	Teacher
19 -	Nursery				
19 -	R				
19 -	Y 1				
19 -	Y 2				
19 -	Y 3				
19 -	Y 4				
19 -	Y 5				
19 -	Y 6				

Figure 3

A Sample of Assessment related to a Statement of Attainment

AT 1 Pupils should:		Y1 E S A	Y2 E S A	Y3 E S A	Y4 E S A	Y5 E S A	Y6 E S A
1 a 1	react to sensory stimulation (without localising the source).						
1 a 2	localise source of sensory stimulation; repeat an action which has an interesting environmental effect.						
1 a 3	show interest in/explore some materials and events in their immediate environment.						
1 a 4	attend to with interest objects and substances and shift attention from one subject/substance to another. Turns / examines object to find appropriate/functional side.						
1 a 5	explore and use with purpose equipment in the indoor and outdoor environments. Show interest in events throughout the school day, recognising environmental clues in context.						
1 a 6	use all their senses to assist their observation of familiar materials and events.						
1 a	observe familiar materials and events.						

KEY

E experience: a pupil has participated in this area of learning, reacting to the experiences and opportunities offered.
S study: a pupil has spent time working at the milestone level in a variety of situations but is not consistent in their achievement.
A achieve: a pupil shows a consistent achievement in this area in a variety of situations.

Figure 4

Conclusion

The National Curriculum document for Science (NCC 1992) states in the programme of study, key stage 1, that:

> *'Pupils should find out about themselves and develop their ideas about how they grow, feed, move and use their senses and about the stages of human development.'*

Also that:

> *'Pupils should consider similarities and differences between themselves and other pupils and understand that individuals are unique.'*

These simple and comprehensive statements describe exactly the emphasis which we have addressed throughout this document, and can equally be applied to adults in relation to accessing opportunities for **ALL** members of society to develop personally and socially, within the framework of learning opportunities which take into account the variations in development and character of each individual. Children and young people who have special educational needs owing to their severe or complex learning difficulties, merely vary in comparison to other individuals, in that they need to overcome a greater number of obstacles than people who do not have a disability.

This document demonstrates a practical framework to enable the children and young people under consideration to:

be scientists

from their earliest experiences, and to participate in the same curriculum as their peers, given the appropriate human and material resources, and a pace and learning style which takes into account the obstacles which they might encounter, in comparison to many of their peers.

We hope that this revised version of 'Science for All' will assist you along that route.

Page 74

Bibliography

Ackerman, D., Mount, H. *Literacy for All*. London: David Fulton.

Aherne, P., Thornber, A., Fagg, S. and Skelton, S. (1990a) *Communication for All*. London: David Fulton.

Aherne, P., Thornber, A., Fagg, S. and Skelton, S. (1990b) *Mathematics for All*. London: David Fulton.

Ashdown et al (Eds) *National Curriculum for pupils with Learning difficulties*. pub. Falmer Press.

Association for Science Education (1988) *The National Curriculum – making it work for the primary school*. Hatfield: ASE.

Bell, P., (1990) *Practical Topics for the Primary School: Science and Technology*, Topical Resources, Preston.

Brent LEA (1989/91) *I can do that* and *I can do that Two*. Primary Science Centre, Birchen Grove, Kingsbury, London NW9 8RY, 1989, 1991.

DES (1985) *Science 5–16: A statement of policy*. London: HMSO.

East Sussex County Council (1990) *We Can All Learn Science*. Richard Read, Education Department, PO Box 4 County Hall, St Anne's Crescent, Lewes BN7 1SG.

Fagg, S., Aherne, P., Skelton, S. and Thornber, A. (1990) *Entitlement for All in Practice*. London: David Fulton.

Howe, L., (1990) *Collins Primary Science*.

Howe, L. (1991) Approaches to Science in: The Curriculum Challenge: Access to the Humberside LEA (1990) Access to Science for Pupils with Special Educational Needs Key stages 1 and 2. Curriculum and Professional Development Unit, Hull Education Centre, Coronation Rd North, Hull HU5 5RL.

Humberside LEA (1991) Access to Science for Pupils with Special Educational Needs Key stages 3 and 4. Curriculum and Professional Development Unit, Hull Education Centre, Coronation Rd North, Hull HU5 5RL.

Jones, A. V. (1990) *Science Education For Pupils With Special Needs*. Nottingham Polytechnic: Nottingham.

Jones, A. Purnell R (1992) *Science: The Physical World, Science: The Living World, Science: The Material World*. Folens Publishers, Albert House, Apex Business Centre, Boscombe Road, Dunstable LU5 4RL. Tel 0528 472575.

Jordan, R. *The National Curriculum – Access for Pupils with Autism*. London: Inge Wakehurst Trst.

Kiernan, C. and Jones, M. (1982) *The Behaviour Assessment Battery*, Windsor: NFER.

Leicestershire County Council (1991) *Steps to Success: Science for pupils with special educational Needs*. Education Offices, County Hall, Glenfield, Leicester LE3 8RF.

Longhorn, F. (1988) *A Sensory Curriculum for Very Special People*. London: Souvenir Press.

MEC (1989a) *Me and My Things*. Manchester: City Council Education Department.

MEC (1989b) *Me and Others*. Manchester: City Council Education Department.

MEC (1989c) *Me and My World*. Manchester: City Council Education Department.

MEC (1989d) *Me and My Surroundings*. Manchester: City Council Education Department.

MEC (1990) *Me and My Movements*, Manchester City Council Education Dept.

MEC (1992) *First Steps to Curriculum Organisation in Primary Schools*. Manchester City Council Education Dept.

MEC peripatetic service (undated) *The Programme Planner for Blind and Partially Sighted Children of Lower Ability*. Manchester: South Manchester Resources Centre.

Mount, H. Ackerman, D. (1991) *Technology for All*. London: David Fulton.

National Curriculum Council (1989b) *Science in the National Curriculum*. London: HMSO.

National Curriculum Council (1989c) *Science: NonStatutory Guidance*. York NCC.

NCC (1990) *A Curriculum for All*, Curriculum Guidance 2.

NCC (1990) NCC Inset Resources.

NCC (1991) *Science and Pupils with Special Educational Needs.* A workshop pack for key stages 1 and 2.

NCC (1992) The National Curriculum and pupils with Severe Learning Difficulties, Curriculum Guidance 9.

NCC (1992) The National Curriculum and pupils with Severe Learning Difficulties Inset Resources.

NCC (1992) Teaching Science to Pupils with Special Educational Needs Curriculum Guidance 10.

National Curriculum Monitoring Group, West Midlands (1989) Broadsheet Number 3 Science, University of Birmingham, School Of Education, PO Box 363, Birmingham B15 2TT, 1990.

SEAC (1989) *SEAC Recorder Number 2*. London: HMSO.

Simon, G.B. (1987) *The Next Step on the Ladder*. Kidderminster: BIMH.

Wren Spinney School (1990) *Modules on level 1 Science.* Westover Road, Ketting, Northants NN16 0AP.

Specialist Science Trolley for pupils with physical disabilities – Var Tech Unit 7, Premier Mill, Begonia Street, Darwen, Lancs. BB3 2DP 0254 773524.

References

Betts, F. (1992) Chemistry for Pupils with Visual Impairment in 'Open Chemistry' Ed. Athey. London: Hodder and Stoughton.

Chapmen, E. and Stone, J. (1988) The Visually Handicapped Child in your classroom. Cassell.

Departments of Education and Science (1989) *From Policy to Practice*. London: DES.

East Sussex SLD Schools (1990). *We Can All Learn Science*, National Curriculum Guidelines. East Sussex Education Authority.

Jones, A.V. (1983) *Science for Handicapped Children*. London: Souvenir Press.

Jones, A.V. (1983) *Things to Make and Do in Science and Technology*. London: Souvenir Press.

Lawson H (1992) Practical Record Keeping for Special Schools. David Fulton.

National Curriculum Council (1989) Curriculum Guidance 1. *A Framework for the Primary Curriculum*. York: NCC.

National Curriculum Council (1989) *English in the National Curriculum*. York: NCC.

National Curriculum Council (1989) *Mathematics in the National Curriculum*. York: NCC.

National Curriculum Council (1989) *Technology in the National Curriculum*. York: NCC.

National Curriculum Council (1989b) *Science in the National Curriculum*. London: HMSO.

National Curriculum Council (1989c) *Science: Non-Statutory Guidance*. York: NCC.

National Curriculum Monitoring Group (SLD) West Midlands (1989/90) Broadsheets 1–3. Birmingham: Westhill College.

NCC (1990) A Curriculum for All, Curriculum Guidance 2.

NCC (1990) NCC Inset Resources.

NCC (1991) Science and Pupils with Special Education Needs. A workshop pack for key stages 1 and 2.

NCC (1992) The National Curriculum and pupils with Severe Learning Difficulties, Curriculum Guidance 9.

NCC (1992) The National Curriculum and pupils with Severe Learning Difficulties, Inset Resources.

NCC (1992) Teaching Science to Pupils with Special Educational Needs, Curriculum Guidance 10.

Reid, D.J. and Hodson, D. (1987) *Science for All*. London: Cassell.

Rowlands, D. Holland, C. (1989) *Problem Solving in Primary Science and Technology, Teachers Guide and Childrens Workpack*. London: Hutchinson.

Womack, D. (1988) *Developing Mathematical and Scientific Thinking in Young Children*. London: Cassell.